Timeline of Early UFO Secrecy in The United States

by Chris Stafford

Copyright © 2016

Chris Stafford Books

Alamo, CA 94507

Library of Congress Catalog Number: 2016917137

ISBN: 0692768858

ISBN-13: 978-0692768853

"Better to reign in hell than serve in heaven ..."

'Paradise Lost' – John Milton

TABLE OF CONTENTS

ACKNOWLEDGEMENTS

I would like to thank my wife, Pamela, and my two children for their patience with me while writing and researching this book. I would also like to thank the following friends of mine who share my interest in the subject: Writer Sean Lynch, Jeffrey Upton M.D., Andrew Dobo Ph.D., and Edward Falensky M.S. They have offered good advice and encouraged me to publish this book.

PREFACE

    If you are new to learning about UFOs or if you have a genuine interest in discovering the truth about them you will run into a labyrinth of information and people. Hard facts can be difficult to come by. There a charlatans, pranksters, crazy people, those trying to make money by selling inaccurate books or film, and those creating cults. There is another element involving secrecy, however. Certain branches of The United States intelligence community have for many decades been creating misinformation for the public to consume. Not only have they manufactured hoaxes, but they have seemingly credible witnesses and UFO researchers who mix truth with fiction. It seems that they will do most any thing to keep the public from looking into this subject seriously. If one scans the internet, looks at YouTube, or attends an UFO conference he will experience just how much misinformation there is. It confuses and frustrates us, so it is wise to approach the subject with 'mental filters' and by withholding final judgment. When I did postgraduate studies at Oxford University, Great Britain the professors there stated that one should not make a statement of fact without having the backing documentation. The problem with UFO research is that we find fact mixed with fiction. Much of the original documentation has been changed or removed in an attempt to throw us off the course to the truth. We are left with sifting through the information from the many UFO researchers and trying to match it with what is commonly known to be historical fact. It is difficult to discern the truth tellers from the deceivers without much scrutiny and after much time and experience. Even the thoroughgoing truth tellers have been deceived from time to time. Some of the following facts are based on the 20.000 unclassified military documents related to UFOs, which were discovered through the Freedom of Information Act. Some of the following information is based on facts by other researchers with whom I have some confidence. I may be wrong by trusting some of those facts, although I believe that the whole of the facts will offer a clear picture of how UFO secrecy developed in The United States, the main keeper of the secrecy.

Because of this inevitable consternation I have endeavored to write a book to shortcut the study process and establish a starting point from which people can work. The chronological timeline of historical facts has an overlay of UFO events, political/organizational developments, technological advances, and scientific developments. This should lend credence to how the UFO facts are presented. One will get a sense of when it was realistic to build advanced propulsion and energy systems based on available scientific technology of the time. I am attempting to offer a brief, yet somewhat comprehensive perspective of the early UFO secrecy. It is not a book trying to prove the existence of extraterrestrials by analyzing witness testimony case after case.

I began writing so that I could make sense of all the disparate facts in my head. It ended up being my 'who, what, where, when, and why' of the UFO mystery. This was a discovery process for me. These ideas came about from reading the many books/articles on the subject, attending lectures, meeting and speaking with prominent researchers, watching videos, and doing extensive outside field work over the years. There are no advanced degrees in UFO studies. I believe there is a need for this kind of book for the confused masses, of whom I am a member.

The San Francisco Call

VOLUME LXXX.—NO. 176.   SAN FRANCISCO, MONDAY MORNING, NOVEMBER 23, 1896.   PRI

A WINGED SHIP IN THE SKY.

It Cleaves the Air With Pinions Like a Huge Condor.

ALL SACRAMENTO SEES THE NEW WONDER.

The Inventor's Lawyer Describes the Machine and Says It Is Genuine.

IT WAS SEEN SOARING NEAR SAN JOSE AT MIDNIGHT.

"The Call's" Exclusive Account of the Greatest Invention of the Age Is Now Corroborated by Thousands.

The Great Airship That Is Startling the People of Many Cities. Drawn From Descriptions of the Inventor's Attorney, George D. Collins.

1896 Many UFO sightings in California

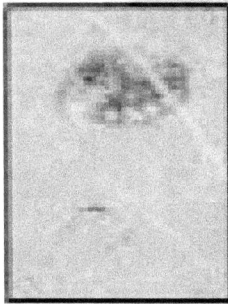
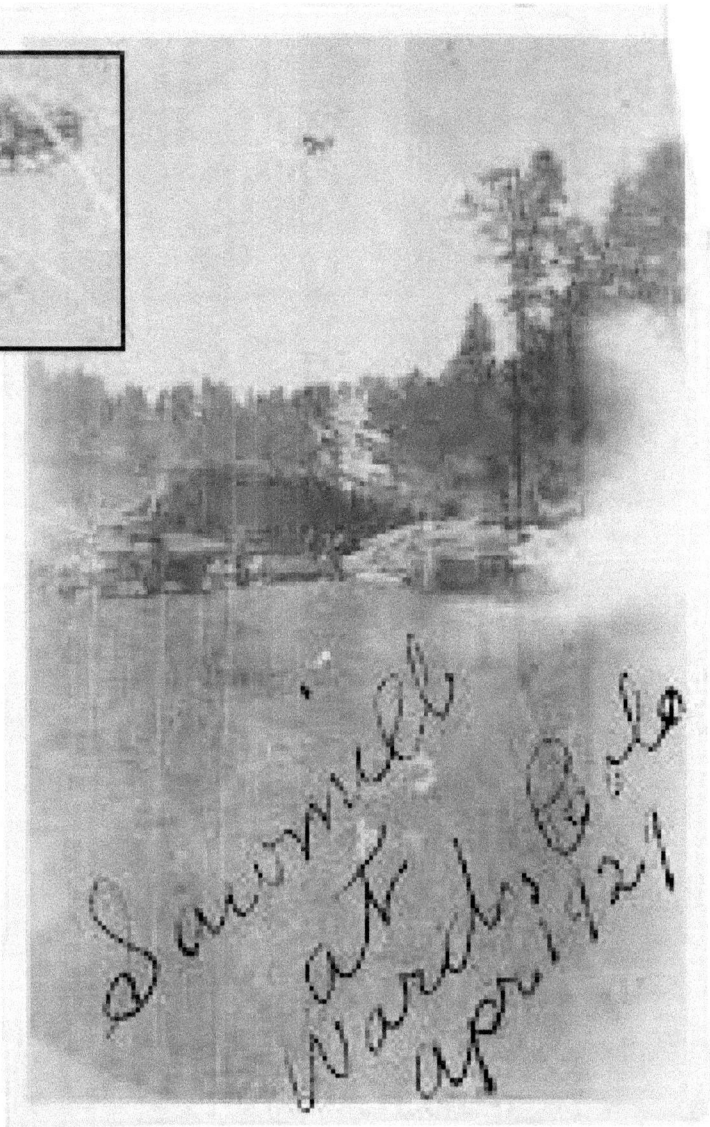

Sawmill at Ward's Cove April 1921

1920's USA

INTRODUCTION

University scientists use the Lambda-CDM Concordance Model and tell us that the universe is roughly 13.798 billion years old. Stephen Hawking claims that our universe came from a singular moment in time. This means that most galaxies, including our Milky Way, are 13.798 billion years old. Using the Hubble Space Telescope cosmologists tell us that there are up to 200 billion observable galaxies in our expanding universe. Our Milky Way Galaxy is of average size and has about 100 to 400 billions stars, according to astronomer David Kornreich. In 2013 astronomers used the Kepler space mission data to project that there are 40 billion earth-sized planets orbiting habitable zones of sun-like stars. Using NASA data, astronomers published a paper for the National Academy of Sciences stating that there are roughly 8.8 billion habitable earth-size planets in our Milky Way Galaxy with suns like ours. Our solar system and our Earth, which are located on it outskirts, are relatively newly formed at roughly 4.54 billion years old, according to radiometric age dating. Dr. Richard Thompson, co-author of the 1993 book, 'Forbidden Archeology,' has discussed finding an artifact from a South African civilization embedded in strata that is three billion years old. DNA researchers, such as Doctor Spencer Wells at Stanford University, say that modern man is about 60,000 years old, and some archeologists say as old as 400,000 years. With statistics such as these it is difficult for one to believe there is no alien life elsewhere. In fact there are those, such as UFO researcher Jacques Vallee, who believe that extraterrestrials have always been with modern man and preceded man. In his 2010 book, 'Wonders in the Sky,' he chronicles UFO events from 1460 BC to the industrial revolution, 1879. English UFO researcher Sir Desmond Leslie stated that UFOs have been landing on earth for thousands of years and offers examples from old manuscripts in his 1952 book, 'Flying Saucers Have Landed.' From early cave paintings, to Ezekiel's wheel, to the flying shields (saucers) Alexander the Great saw while going into battle, history is replete with UFO sightings interpreted within the context of each culture. So too with The United States, having the first government UFO inquiry held in January, 1814 by the 13th congress, second session. In a naval encounter during the War of 1812 UFOs with blue lights appeared above Groton, Connecticut and then above New London Harbor. No conclusion was reached. It is interesting to note that through the 1800s UFO sightings were attributed to newly discovered comets and meteors, despite their zigzag paths and erratic movements. Astronomers of the time, such as Barnard, noticed a spike in comet sightings from 1877 to 1881. This happened to coincide with the early years of the Second Industrial Revolution, including the rapid development of electrical engineering. The earliest documented photograph of an UFO in North America was by a well-known Mexican astronomer named Jose Bonilla in August of 1883. Over a two day period at Zacatecas Observatory he and his assistant were studying the sun's corona when they observed a fleet of 447 "flying discs" flying in various formations about 242,000 kms away. In his reports and also in his article in 'L'Astronomie Magazine' he never suggested that these observations were any type of space debris. America's first ufologist was Charles Fort, who published his first book, 'The Book of The Damned,' in 1919. This book and subsequent books dealt, in part, with UFO reports.

The following 'Timeline of Early UFO Secrecy in The United States' begins with the Franklin D. Roosevelt administration and ends with the Richard M. Nixon administration, from 1933 to 1974. This period was chosen because before FDR's time there were fewer sightings, and no attempt was made for mass secrecy due to a lack of understanding of the UFO phenomenon. It did not fit into the people's worldview of the time and was largely ignored until the fathers of science fiction, Jules Vern and H. G. Wells, wrote their novels in the last half of the 1800s. The Nixon years were chosen as an end point because by 1970 the ruling elite of the Western world, under multinational control, had taken UFO matters into their hands and decided that all UFO information was to be suppressed. They decided that the general public would not share in the knowledge of the extraterrestrial presence or benefit from the related new-found technologies. It was a time when public interest in UFOs was to be reduced, a time when significant programs were implemented to confuse, distract, and disseminate misinformation to the people. This was also a time when U.S. technologies advanced to the point where elaborate hoaxes and deception could be more easily achieved. As a result, there should be greater distrust of UFO information after 1969.

The sudden increase in UFO sightings during and after World War II was attributable to the world's entry into modern warfare. This also included the development of the atomic bomb, nuclear power plants, radar, rockets, satellites, and space travel programs. Extraterrestrial involvement became more pronounced and could not be ignored. An overlay of some of the scientific and technological discoveries is useful in giving perspective as to when the manufacture of advanced propulsion and computer-based systems was possible. The following timeline includes some of the major UFO events of the time, as well as UFO events that caused a response from the government and/or the military. Specific details of an UFO event are less important than how the government and military reacted to the event. My hope is that the reader will see the significant historical cause and effect events that led to how the UFO secrecy evolved in The United States.

Around 1900 Santa Catalina Island, California

1932 St. Paris, Ohio

1942 Tiensten, Hopeh Province, China

1948 Anchorage, Alaska

1952 Passaic, New Jersey

THE TIMELINE

1933, MARCH 4 – Franklin D. Roosevelt becomes the 32nd
President of The United States until his death on April 12, 1945.

1935 – Radar was successfully tested by The United States
Army. This was a primitive surface-to-air radar system, but the
technology was developed and installed in military tracking
stations for aircraft detection by the beginning of World War II,
in 1939.

1936 – The Rural Electrification Act provided federal loans so
that electricity could be installed in areas of the U.S. that did not
have electricity.

1937, JULY 2 - Amelia Earhart disappears in the Pacific Ocean
while trying to fly around the world. The first aerial
circumnavigation of the world was in 1924 by a team of aviators
of The United States Army Air Service. The trip took 175 days.

1938, OCTOBER 31 – Orson Wells broadcasts 'The War of the
Worlds' on the Mercury Theater radio show during Halloween
night to seven million people. Many listeners believed that an
invasion from Mars was actually occurring.

1939 – Secretary of State under FDR, Cordell Hull, shows his
brother, Reverend Hull, and colleague, Reverend Holt, the
bodies of four small aliens preserved in glass jars and a flying
saucer. This was in a room located under the basement of the
U.S. Capitol. It was verified only by Reverend Hull's children
and grandchildren. There were many reports of UFO crashes
through the 1800s and early 1900s. Retired Lieutenant Colonel
Kevin Randle lists some of them in his 2010 book, 'Crash.'

1939, SEPTEMBER 1 – World War II is initiated in Europe
when Germany invades Poland.

1940 – President Roosevelt authorizes the FBI to engage in electronic eavesdropping on suspicious individuals in the American citizenry under the direction of J. Edgar Hoover. This included placing 'bugs,' which required break-ins.

1940 – UFO sightings started to occur with greater frequency all over the world during World War II, especially in Europe. According to UFO researcher Leonard S. Stringfield most sightings were over Germany and Holland before 1942. Other 1940s sightings can be found in UFO researcher Jerome Clark's 'The UFO Encyclopedia: The Phenomenon from the Beginning,' first published in 1990. They were later called "Foo Fighters" in 1944. Military UFO researcher Major Donald Kehoe cataloged hundreds of these military sightings after the war.

1941, APRIL – Cape Girardeau, Missouri UFO/saucer crash occurs. The military takes away a saucer and three dead alien bodies. They tell the town's witnesses not to discuss the incident. The saucer was sent to Purdue University for analysis. The FBI was also involved in the cover-up.

1941, DECEMBER 7 – Pearl Harbor is attacked by the Japanese and The United States declares war the next day.

1942, FEBRUARY 24 – The Battle of Los Angeles occurs. A large UFO hovers over Los Angeles and the military fires over 1400 shells with no effect. One million people woke up to sirens and shooting. There were clams that the UFO caused the black out of the city. Secretary of the Navy, Frank Knox, holds a press conference and says it was a false alarm caused by "war nerves." The military and FDR were not sure of what it was, but the masses saw a giant, silent, hovering flying saucer. Many witnesses also saw multiple smaller alien craft.

1942 FEBRUARY 26 – The Los Angles Times writes a frontpage story, "L.A. Area Raided!" with photos of the craft.

Los Angeles, CA. Feb. 25, 1942

1942 'Battle of Los Angeles' photo

Los Angeles Times

ARMY SAYS ALARM REAL

U.S. Flyers Reap Indies Victories

Storm Grows Over Delay in Alien Ouster

INFORMATION, PLEASE

Five Deaths Laid to Raid Blackout

Roaring Guns Mark Blackout

Rangoon Aces Bag 30 Planes

WAR EXTRA

Los Angeles Examiner

9 A.M. FINAL

AIR BATTLE RAGES OVER LOS ANGELES

IN THE NEWS — Impossible to Send MacArthur Planes, Roosevelt Asserts — RUSSIANS TRAP 48,000 NAZIS, KILL 12,000 — One Plane Reported Downed on Vermont Avenue by Gunfire — HUNT ON FOR SPIES ALONG NIPPON SUB

1942, JUNE 13 – The Office of Strategic Services (OSS) is formed at the request of President Roosevelt. He asked William J. Donavan to create an organization similar to Great Britain's Secret Intelligence Service (MI6) and Specials Operation Executive (SOE). This was the predecessor to the CIA with the purpose of coordinating espionage activities between the U.S. military branches. They also did propaganda, subversion, and post-war planning while reporting to the Joint Chiefs of Staff. Allen Dulles was an OSS officer and was part of 'Operation Paperclip.' The U.S. National Archives released the names of many of its OSS members on August 14, 2008. Among the names were officer Clay Shaw of the JFK assassination investigation, chef Julia Child, author Arthur Schlesinger Jr., director John Ford, statesman Arthur Goldberg, and baseball player Moe Berg.

1943 – Interplanetary Phenomenon Unit (IPU) was created by General Douglas MacArthur to investigate the UFO sightings around the world and set up UFO retrieval teams. The existence of this unit was confirmed by four independent UFO researchers and their government sources (Richard Hall, William Steinman, Clifford Stone, and Timothy Good). Jimmy Doolittle was part of this group and reported to General MacArthur in response to the many UFO sightings during WWII. They worked with the Army Counter Intelligence Corps (CIC), later to become the USAF OSI. Their findings in 1943 were that the "foo fighters" were interplanetary craft visiting earth to observe World War II. This was to have been found in a 10,000 page report given to the Joint Chiefs of Staff in the late 1940s. The report was a compilation of the many military reports during the war, but a copy has never surfaced. According to UFO presidential researcher Grant Cameron, President Truman commissioned a study of "foo fighters" in 1949 headed by General Jimmy Doolittle. Doolittle stated that the Germans may have had a crashed UFO as early as 1939. The study results gave them great concern about what the UFO objectives could be. General MacArthur was to have understood this and was to have seen the hard evidence of crashed UFOs, including the later Roswell crash debris. This organization, the IPU, was later taken over by General George C. Marshall and still exists today, although the various retrieval projects have changed names through the years. Sergeant Clifford Stone explains this in detail in his 2011 book, 'Eyes Only.' Stone claims he was part of the retrieval teams from the late 1960s until 1990. By 1969, he claims, they had retrieved about 24 UFO craft. Researcher Leonard Stringfield claims there were 35 worldwide UFO crash/retrieval events from WWII to 1969. Fifteen of the 35 UFO crashes were in 1952 and 1953. Other sources, such as General MacArthur's personal security guard, have corroborated the MacArthur information.

1943 – Production of the first V-2 rocket in Germany began. This was the first long range rocket capable of carrying 2200 pounds a distance of 190 miles. It eventually evolved into the American Redstone Rocket used in the early U.S. space program. It was developed by German scientists, including Wernher von Braun, who came to America after WWII through the 'Operation Paper Clip' program.

1944 and 1945 – "Foo Fighters" were seen over Europe and Japan during WWII flights. They were officially reported and named in 1944. Most sightings were of UFO orbs, and the military were not sure of what they were. The Air Force explained that these were hallucinations caused by pilot fatigue. This was their common debunking explanation in the earliest years. Researcher Major Donald Keyhoe collected information of the sightings from hundreds of pilots.

1945, APRIL 12 – Harry S. Truman becomes the 33rd President of The United States until January 20, 1953. President Roosevelt did not have a clear understanding of the UFO phenomenon before his death on April 12th, 1945.

1945, JANUARY 2 – The New York Times publishes the story, 'Balls of Fire Stalk U.S. Fighters in Night Assaults over Germany.'

WWII Foo Fighters

1943 Japanese Sea Foo Fighter

Floating Mystery Ball Is New Nazi Air Weapon

SUPREME HEADQUARTERS, Allied Expeditionary Force, Dec. 13—A new German weapon has made its appearance on the western air front, it was disclosed today.

Airmen of the American Air Force report that they are encountering silver colored spheres in the air over German territory. The spheres are encountered either singly or in clusters. Sometimes they are semi-translucent.

SUPREME HEADQUARTERS, Dec. 13 (Reuter)—The Germans have produced a "secret" weapon in keeping with the Christmas season.

The new device, apparently an air defense weapon, resembles the huge glass balls that adorn Christmas trees.

There was no information available as to what holds them up like stars in the sky, what is in them, or what their purpose is supposed to be.

1945, MAY 2 – Germany surrenders to the allies in WWII. All of German technology facilities are in shambles.

1945, JULY 16 – The world's first atomic bomb detonation occurs, code name 'Trinity,' at White Sands Proving Ground Facility, New Mexico. It was developed through the Manhattan Project and was a plutonium implosion fission device yielding the equivalent of 20 kilotons of TNT.

1945, AUGUST 6 and 9 – Truman drops two atomic bombs on the Japanese cities of Nagasaki and Hiroshima. UFOs are spotted by some chronicling the event.

1945, AUGUST 15 – Japan surrenders to the allies in WWII.

1945, AUGUST 28 – Leonard H. Stringfield, then an Army Air Force intelligence officer, encountered three teardrop-shaped white objects on a clear day flying parallel to their C-46 plane to Iwa Jima. This event inspired him to spend the rest of his life researching UFOs. He created the Civilian Research of Interplanetary Objects (CRIFO) and published monthly news letters called 'ORBIT.' It became the world's largest UFO research group of its day. He also published many papers and books, but his specialty was collecting witness accounts of government retrievals of alien bodies after UFO crashes. In 1957 he became public relations advisor for NICAP and became friends with Major Donald Keyhoe. Later he became a board member for MUFON and a regional director for the J. Allen Hynek Center for UFO Studies.

1945, AUGUST – 'Operation Paperclip' was created through executive order by President Truman. This was an Office of Strategic Services (OSS) program conducted by the Joint Intelligence Objectives Agency (JIOA), which was a subcommittee of the Joint Intelligence Committee of the Joint Chiefs of Staff. The operation brought 1500 scientists, technicians, and engineers from post-war Germany to The United States for employment. The JIOA falsified papers and hid any Nazi involvement. Among the rocket scientists was renowned engineer Wernher von Braun. They were at the heart of the U.S. rocket program going forward.

1945, SEPTEMBER 20 – The OSS disbanded by executive order 9621 under President Truman. By this time they had done their own investigation of "Foo Fighters" and determined that they were not German experimental craft. It is true that the Germans were working on disc shaped flying objects, but there is no hard evidence that they worked effectively and contributed to the war effort. One example is the German inventor, Viktor Shauberger, who was to have been commissioned by the SS. Some researchers have claimed that he or other engineers were to have back engineered a supposed crashed UFO found in the Black Forest in the late 1930s. At any rate, Shauberger later stated that manufacturing techniques and building materials of the time were not advanced enough to produce a flying saucer using his advanced ideas, such as 'the repulsin.' All of his prototypes were small in size.

1945, OCTOBER 1 – Bureau of Intelligence and Research, INR, is created. It was previously under the Office of Strategic Services from 1942 to 1945. It was now under the Secretary of State and provided intelligence to ambassadors, embassy staff, and other policy makers.

1946, JANUARY – The National Intelligence Authority (NIA) is formed under the direction of President Truman as a central intelligence group coordinating all intelligence headed by Rear Admiral Sidney Souers, Deputy Chief of Naval Intelligence. This included the Secretary of State, the Secretary of War, and the Secretary of the Navy Chief of Staff. The CIG was part of this organization.

1946, JUNE 10 – The Central Intelligence Group (CIG) is headed by Hoyt Vandenberg. He came from the Army as Director of Intelligence.

1946, JULY 8 – The first detonation of Pacific Proving Grounds testing occurred at Bikini Atoll, Marshal Islands. There were

105 above ground detonations that occurred until 1962. That was 80% of all U.S. detonation yields. UFOs/saucers were seen and recorded during the blasts.

1946, AUGUST 1 – The Atomic Energy Act of 1946 is signed by Truman, which then creates the Atomic Energy Commission. "Unexpectedly high costs in the Second World War nuclear weapons program created pressure on federal officials to develop a civilian nuclear power industry that could help justify the government's considerable expenditures." This was why the safer avenues of energy research were not pursued, according to the 1996 book, 'Governing the Atom: The politics of Risk,' by Byrne and Hoffman.

1946, AUGUST 26 – Admiral Byrd heads 'Operation High Jump' to Antarctica under the orders of Secretary of Navy James Forrestal. Byrd takes an armada of thirteen war ships, 4700 men, and multiple aircraft. The public is told that its mission is to establish an Antarctic research base and train the Navy in the arctic. Byrd leaves early on 2/28/47 because of encounters with flying objects. He reports to the International News Service, first in Argentina, then in Chile's El Mercurio Newpaper, that " The United States should adopt measures of protection against the possibility of an invasion of the country by hostile planes coming from the polar regions." He expressed his deep concern for the security of The United States, but never mentions a German base or German flying saucers with anti-gravity propulsion. There is no evidence that the Germans ever settled in Antarctica, although they did fly over and drop small Nazi flags. If Hitler would have had these flying saucers, or the atomic bomb for that matter, Hitler would have used them. The Navy then forbids Byrd from discussing this at future press conferences or lecturing about the topic. He is declared mentally unstable. His son, an Harvard graduate and naval officer, dies on route to speak at a National Geographic Society event honoring his father's 100th birthday in Washington D.C. in 1988. His son was also declared mentally unstable. Some of the future Antarctic expeditions also see UFOs.

1946 Operation High Jump

Operation High Jump

El almirante Richard E. Byrd se refiere a la importancia estratégica de los polos

The "El Mercurio" Article Citing Admiral Byrd's Remarks

Admiral Byrd's Santiago, Chilean newspaper article

1946, SEPTEMBER – The Army's Signal Security Agency persuaded ITT, RCA, and Western Union to continue the wartime cable intercept program, code name 'Shamrock.' They targeted everyone, foreign and domestic, for 30 years.

1946, DECEMBER – Life and Newsweek magazines publish articles explaining how German scientists are now working for the U.S. at Wright Air Force Base in Dayton, Ohio.

1947, JANUARY 1 – The Atomic Energy Commission takes control of atomic energy in the U.S. This transfers control from the military to civilian hands, but utilizes all of the military resources used in WWII to further develop the atomic bomb.

1947, MAY 1 – Rear Admiral Roscoe H. Hillenkoetter becomes the director of the CIG. It is a puzzlement that he was later on the NICAP board of directors from 1957 to 1962, and was a colleague of Major Donald Kehoe.

1947, JUNE AND JULY – There was a significant increase in UFO sightings all over the United States. Before the Kenneth Arnold sighting there were concentrated sightings in Delaware, Washington, Iowa, and California.

1947, JUNE – Oak Ridge Nuclear Facility in Tennessee has a series of UFO sightings. This was an atomic testing facility for the Atomic Energy Commission, housing some of the world's most sophisticated technology.

1947, JUNE 24 – Pilot Kenneth Arnold has a sighting of nine flying saucers in Washington State by Mount Rainier flying at 1700 MPH. This is the first time the term, "flying saucer," is used. Arnold has later UFO sightings and does his own UFO research for the rest of his life. He was disturbed at why the U.S. government did not focus on disclosure to the people. His 1952 book, 'The Coming of The Saucers,' discusses the Maury Island cover-up as well as his experience and research.

Pilot Kenneth Arnold

WESTERN UNION

To: Commanding General
Wright Field
Dayton, Ohio

Dear Sir:

You have my permission to quote, give out, or reprint my written account and report of nine strange aircraft I observed on June 24th, in the Cascade Mountains in the State of Washington. This report was sent to you at request some days ago. It is with considerable disappointment you cannot give the explanation of these aircraft as I felt certain they belonged to our government. They have apparently meant no harm, but used as an instrument of destruction in combination with our atomic bomb the effects could destroy life on our planet. Capt. Smith, co-pilot, Stevens of United Air Lines, and myself have compared our observations in as much detail as possible, and agreed we had observed the same type of Aircraft as to size, shape and form.

We have not taken this lightly. It is to us of very serious concern. As we are as interested in the welfare of our country as you are.

Boise, Idaho
Pilots License 333487
Kenneth Arnold

Kenneth Arnold's message to Wright Field

1947, JULY 8 – Roswell crashes occur and there are many early military documents referring to this as a major event that upset the military. One military document states that it was the same type of craft and alien beings as an earlier crash. There were two crashed flying saucers with injured and dead extraterrestrial beings. The location of the second crash was 250 miles away in St. Augusta. Air Force's General Nathan Twining oversees the event and has the bodies, now called the Greys, and saucer debris sent to Wright-Patterson AFB. Roswell researcher Stanton Friedman shows compelling information in his video of 27 Roswell witnesses called, 'Recollections of Roswell,' copyright 1992. His 1997 book, 'Crash at Corona: The Definitive Story of the Roswell Incident,' goes into further detail. Friedman states that New Mexico, at that time, was the only place where advanced propulsion systems, experimental radar, and nuclear weapon research was going on simultaneously.

1947, JULY 8 – The Roswell Daily Record prints the frontpage article, 'RAAF Captures Flying Saucer on Ranch in Roswell Region.'

1947, JULY 9 – Brigadier General George Schulgen, Chief of Air Intelligence Requirements Division of the Army Corps Intelligence, asks the FBI to investigate 'saucer' reports.

1947, JULY 11 - J. Edgar Hoover responds to Brigadier General George Schulgen's request and is quoted as saying, " I would do it (study UFOs), but before agreeing to do it, we must insist upon full access to discs recovered. For instance in the L.A. case (Los Alamos/Roswell), the Army grabbed it and would not let us have it for cursory examination." This quote is accurate according to the research by Dr. Bruce Maccabee, ufologist.

Roswell Daily Record

RAAF Captures Flying Saucer On Ranch in Roswell Region

Claims Army Is Stacking Courts Martial

GRAND

House Passes Tax Slash by Large Margin

Security Council Paves Way to Talks On Arms Reductions

No Details of Flying Disk Are Revealed

Harassed Rancher who Located 'Saucer' Sorry He Told About It

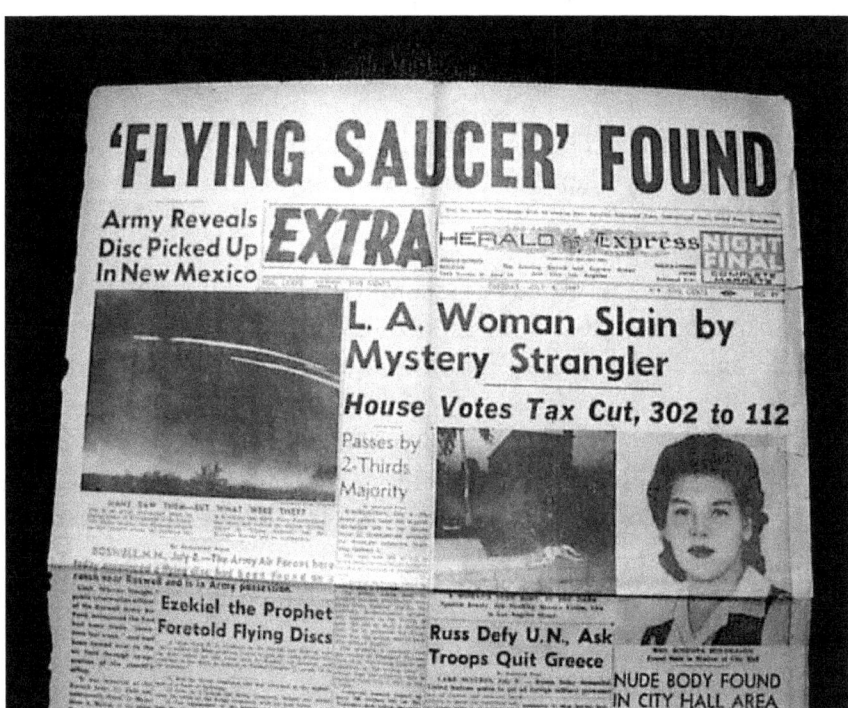

'FLYING SAUCER' FOUND

Army Reveals Disc Picked Up In New Mexico

EXTRA

HERALD Express

NIGHT FINAL

L. A. Woman Slain by Mystery Strangler

House Votes Tax Cut, 302 to 112

Passes by 2-Thirds Majority

Ezekiel the Prophet Foretold Flying Discs

Russ Defy U.N. Ask Troops Quit Greece

NUDE BODY FOUND IN CITY HALL AREA

I would do it [study UFOs], but before agreeing to do it, we must insist upon full access to discs recovered. For instance in the L.A. case, the Army grabbed it and would not let us have it for cursory examination.

— J. Edgar Hoover —

AZ QUOTES

The Air Force kept the FBI at a distance after Roswell

1947, JULY 21 & 22 – The Maury Island UFO crash happens on Puget Sound, Washington State. Six 100 feet donut shaped saucers are spotted by two fishermen. They recover debris spilled while the saucers hover. 'Men in black' show up and threaten to kill them and their families if anything is said, according to the fisherman.

1947, JULY 26 – Truman creates the National Security Act through which the CIA, Central Intelligence Agency, is formed (officially September 18, 1947). Truman also puts the four branches of the military under the new Secretary of Defense, James Forrestal. Some researchers have called this the beginning of the 'shadow government.' This unified the National Military Establishment (NME), the National Security Council (NSC), and the Central Intelligence Agency (CIA).

1947, AUGUST 1 – The Air Force splits from the Army. The Army Corps and the Army Counter Intelligence Corps (CIC) go to the Air Force. The day before there is a crash of a B-52 killing U.S. Army intelligence officers and pilots Davidson and Brown. They were on route to deliver debris and information from the Maury Island Crash. There were only two other crew members on board, but they parachuted to safety. Donald Keyhoe wrote that there was much anger and competitiveness between the military branches concerning who would control the UFO phenomenon before that time. All branches of the military were working on the UFO problem up to this point, although the Air Force had the lead.

1947, SEPTEMBER 23 – General Nathan Twining, head of Air Material Command, overseer of the Roswell incident, writes a classified military letter regarding flying discs as, "real and not visionary or fictitious." He also stated openly that UFOs are not secret American craft.

1947, SEPTEMBER 24 – Truman, by executive order, has James Forrestal create a secret committee of scientists, military leaders, and government officials called MJ-12 (Majestic). According to Wilbert Smith from Canada's 'Project Magnet' the purpose of the group was to look into the physics and technology of UFOs, headed by Dr. Vannevar Bush. Among the alleged, original twelve members included General Nathan Twining, General Hoyt Vandenburg, Secretary of Defense James Forrestal, CIA Director Admiral Roscoe Hillenkoetter, Dr. Jerome Bronk, Dr. Jerome Hunsucker, Dr. Lloyd Berkner, General Robert Montague, Assistant Secretary of the Army Gordan Gray, Rear Admiral Sidney Souers, and Dr. Donald Menzel. There was no government oversight for this group, and they participated in the cover-up strategy. One example was Dr. Donald Menzel writing debunking books and his later testimony at the 1968 congressional hearings to debunk the UFO phenomenon. Menzel was a noted astronomer and astrophysicist. Researchers say that this is the group, possibly under another name, that took over the UFO information and aligned with 'the military-industrial complex.' President Eisenhower eventually realized that he had lost control of the group and was kept in the dark during his presidency.

1947, OCTOBER 1 – The Air Force formally ends cooperation with the FBI in investigating UFOs, but the FBI continues investigating on its own.

1947, OCTOBER 14 – The sound barrier is broken by Chuck Yeager at Muroc AFB, now Edwards AFB. He flew the X-1 768 miles per hour, Mach 1, at an altitude of 45,000 feet.

1947 – The first bipolar transistor was invented and replaced vacuum tubes after 1955 in computer designs.

1947, DECEMBER – Bell Labs gets credit for discovering the transistor. Much of the research had already been done at Purdue University from 1941 to 1945 and some physicists believe that Purdue should have gotten credit. Purdue's department of physics staff grew from eleven in 1945 to 62 by the early 1970s. They were the leaders in particle physics among all universities in the 1940s and 1950s and were supported by the Atomic Energy Commission.

September 24, 1947.

MEMORANDUM FOR THE SECRETARY OF DEFENSE

Dear Secretary Forrestal:

As per our recent conversation on this matter, you are hereby authorized to proceed with all due speed and caution upon your undertaking. Hereafter this matter shall be referred to only as Operation Majestic Twelve.

It continues to be my feeling that any future considerations relative to the ultimate disposition of this matter should rest solely with the Office of the President following appropriate discussions with yourself, Dr. Bush and the Director of Central Intelligence.

[signature]

Truman's letter to James Forrestal

Some of the original members of MJ-12 from left to right:

General Nathan Twining, General Hoyt Vandenberg, James
Forrestal, Admiral Sidney Souers?

1947, DECEMBER 30 – Project Sign is created by order of Air Force Major General Laurence C. Craigie. General Nathan Twining is in charge to "collect, collate, evaluate, and distribute to interested government agencies and contractors all information concerning sightings and phenomena in the atmosphere which can be construed to be of concern to national security." The Air Force also used Project Sign to debunk UFO sightings with the public. They used astronomers, astrophysicists, rocket experts, technical analysts, Air Force Special Intelligence, and the FBI. The director was Captain Robert R. Sneider, and it was set up under the Air Materiel Command at Wright-Patterson AFB in Dayton, Ohio. They also called it Project Saucer. A contingent of analysts at Wright-Patterson were called the Air Technical Intelligence Center (ATIC), and some of them believed that the UFOs were extraterrestrial.

1948 – An 'Estimate of the Situation' report is created by Project Sign and presented to the high command and General Hoyt Vandenberg. It states that the UFOs were believed to be interplanetary and that public disclosure was recommended. It also stated that aliens were making a full-scale observation of earth, but that an attack did not seem imminent. Major Dewey Fournet and Captain Edward Ruppelt claimed to have seen and read the document. General Vandenberg decided not to have public disclosure of the information and ordered all copies of the report to be destroyed.

1948 AUGUST 1 – The Office of Special Investigations (AFOSI and OSI) is created in the Air Force. They took over primary UFO investigations and retrieval teams. Some of their results were given to Project Sign, eventually called Project Blue Book, in a watered down version. They also monitored the UFO research at Wright-Patterson AFB. UFO researcher Bill Moore, member of NICAP and APRO, claims that these are the 'men in black (MIB).' Any previous MIB came from the pre 1947 Army/USAF special unit created in 1943. There are reports throughout the world of MIB looking into UFO sightings and phenomenon. MUFON has over 100 reports going back to the 1950s with MIB using extreme intimidation and threats to silence UFO witnesses. Some researchers today also claim the MIB sometimes come from the CIA, NSA, and other military intelligence groups.

1948, SEPTEMBER 3 – The first nuclear reactor generates electricity at the X-10 reactor located in Oak Ridge, Tennessee.

1948, OCTOBER 1 – The 'Gorman UFO Dogfight' occurs over Fargo, North Dakota. Captain Edward Ruppelt believed that this incident and two others the same year proved to the USAF that UFOs were real. In 1949 the USAF called the sightings weather balloons.

1948, DECEMBER 29 – James Forrestal releases an official statement, "The Earth Satellite Vehicle Program, which is being carried out independently by each military service, has been assigned to the Committee on Guided missiles for co-ordination."

1949 – Significant sightings of UFOs, including "green fireballs," occur around vital research and military installations, especially around Los Alamos, New Mexico (near Roswell). This is where American atomic bombs were being designed. By the end of 1948 there were 50 bombs stored there.

1949, FEBRUARY – Project Grudge replaces Project Sign and is created by the Air Force to debunk UFO sightings because Project Sign was not aggressive enough. Many military personnel involved with Project Sign wanted public disclosure, but Chief of Staff, General Hoyt Vandenberg, would not permit it. Many respected objective scientists affiliated with both programs resigned. As stated earlier, Vandenberg's decision was made after reading the top secret document on August 5, 1948 from Project Sign called, 'Estimate of the Situation.'

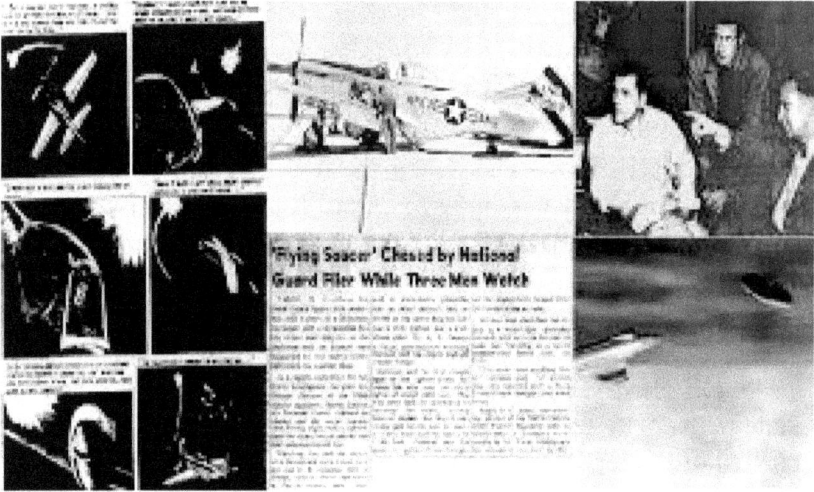

1948 Gorman UFO dogfight

Office Memorandum · UNITED STATES GOVERNMENT

TO : DIRECTOR, FBI

DATE: January 31, 1949

FROM : SAC, SAN ANTONIO

SUBJECT: PROTECTION OF VITAL INSTALLATIONS
BUREAU FILE # 65-58300

CONFIDENTIAL declassified
2010 8/31/77

At recent Weekly Intelligence Conferences of G-2, ONI, OSI, and F.B.I., in the Fourth Army Area, Officers of G-2, Fourth Army have discussed the matter of "Unidentified Aircraft" or "Unidentified Aerial Phenomena" otherwise known as "Flying Discs", "Flying Saucers", and "Balls of Fire". This matter is considered top secret by Intelligence Officers of both the Army and the Air Forces.

It is well known that there have been during the past two years reports from the various parts of the country of the sighting of unidentified aerial objects which have been called in newspaper parlance "flying discs" and "flying saucers". The first such sightings were reported from Sweden, and it was thought that the objects, the nature of which was unknown, might have originated in Russia.

In July 1948 an unidentified aircraft was "seen" by an Eastern Airlines pilot and Co-Pilot and one or more passengers of the Eastern Airlines Plane over Montgomery, Alabama. This aircraft was reported to be of an unconventional type without wings and resembled generally a "rocket ship" of the type depicted in comic strips. It was reported to have had windows; to have been larger than the Eastern Airlines plane, and to have been traveling at an estimated speed of 2700 miles an hour. It appeared out of a thunderhead ahead of the Eastern Airlines plane and immediately disappeared in another cloud narrowly missing a collision with the Eastern Airlines plane. No sound or air disturbance was noted in connection with this appearance.

During the past two months various sightings of unexplained phenomena have been reported in the vicinity of the A.E.C. Installation at Los Alamos, New Mexico, where these phenomena now appear to be concentrated. During December 1948 on the 5th, 6th, 7th, 8th, 11th, 13, 14th, 20th and 28th sightings of unexplained phenomena were made near Los Alamos by Special Agents of the Office of Special Investigation; Airline Pilots; Military Pilots, Los Alamos Security Inspectors, and private citizens. On January 6, 1949, another similar object was sighted in the same area.

b7c ████████████ a Meteorologist of some note, has been generally in charge of the observations near Los Alamos, attempting to learn characteristics of the unexplained phenomena.

Up to this time little concrete information has been obtained.

JEJ:md
S.-100-7545
cc: El Paso (2)
Dallas (2)
Houston (2)
Little Rock (2)
Oklahoma City (2)

RECORDED

F B I
13 MAR 16 1949

1949 Los Alamos UFO sightings reported to the FBI

Held at 1300, 16 February 1949, in conference room P-162, Los Alamos
Scientific Laboratory, Los Alamos, New Mexico. Present:

4th Army:	Major Winn
	Major Godsoe
	Captain Neef
AFSWP:	Commander Mandelkorn
University of New Mexico:	Dr. LaPaz
FBI:	Mr. Maxwell
USAEC, SFOO:	Mr. Morgan
	Mr. Newburger
University of California:	Dr. Bradbury
	Dr. Holloway
	Mr. Hoyt
	Dr. Manley
	Dr. Reines
	Dr. Teller

Mr. Newburger opened the conference and stated that the subject of Aerial
Phenomena was classified Secret within the meaning of AR 380-5 and comparable
appropriate regulations of the Navy and Air Forces, and that all personnel at
this meeting were properly cleared. Mr. Newburger then introduced Captain
Neef, who briefly outlined the purpose of this meeting.

Captain Neef: It all started back in December, 1948, when we first received
some reports from some airline pilots that these green fireballs were sighted.
At this stage we had no idea what to do with it or what it was. We approached
Dr. LaPaz who has been assisting us, gratis, since that date. Almost over two
months now that he has been assisting us, so in order to have you get the facts
as they are to a scientist, I'll let Dr. LaPaz explain these things as we have
found them. Then you can give us your opinion from there; that is what we are
interested in.

Dr. LaPaz: I would like to review what is observed in the case of a conventional meteorite fall. Not that I have any hopes of saying anything you
don't already know, but because I regard the observational evidence observed
by the conventional meteorite falls as providing the necessary background
for what is now observed. Meteorite falls (for next minute or two, Dr.
LaPaz's comments on record drowned out by noise from ditch digger immediately
outside conference room)....Because of sound phenomena primarily, the fall
of a large meteorite will cause great fright among human beings necessarily
but primarily among animals, of all kinds. The fact follows, by a meteorite

1949, MARCH THROUGH JUNE – Camp Hood, now Fort Hood, Texas has ongoing sightings of various types of craft. This was when Camp Hood had the largest stockpile of nuclear weapons in the country. As many as 50 sightings per night were seen by hundreds of military witnesses. All branches of the military were involved in this investigation, but the Air Force silenced all reports.

1949, March 31 – Truman asks for James Forrestal's resignation because of Forrestal's lack of loyalty. Forrestal feels the public should know about UFOs, and some researchers claim that Forrestal saw the alien bodies from the Roswell crash.

1949, APRIL 27 – A government report is published, approved by Forrestal, discussing "space visitors."

1949, MAY 22 – James Forrestal commits suicide after previously being declared mentally unstable. He jumped out of his sixteenth floor window at Bethesda Naval Hospital. His family members suspected foul play and his brother, Henry, had a very strong belief that he was murdered.

1949, JUNE 8 – George Orwell publishes his novel, 'Nineteen Eighty-Four,' about "big brother" controlling the masses with extensive secretive surveillance and the "thought police." "Big brother" was the elite ruling class comprised of less than two percent of the world's population. 85% of the population is poor and dependent on the government in this novel with the remainder of the people as part of the governing class.

1949, SEPTEMBER – The Soviet Union detonates its first nuclear weapon, which accelerated The United States development of its own nuclear weapon program, as ordered by President Truman. This was the beginning of the nuclear arms race with Russia. By the late 1970s there were seven nations with hydrogen bombs.

1949, DECEMBER 6 – Project Grudge puts out their final
report after reviewing 244 cases. It firmly debunks UFO
sightings and gives four reasons for the sightings:
1. Psychopathic behavior
2. Hoaxes
3. Mass Hysteria
4. Misinterpretation

1950, MARCH – Guy Hottel, the SAC for Washington State
reports to the FBI that three fifty foot diameter saucers crashed
and had been recovered in New Mexico with nine three foot tall
alien bodies.

The Hottel Memorandum

1950, JUNE 25 – The Korean War starts and ends on July 27th, 1953. General Douglas MacArthur is Supreme Commander in Korea and is excessive in his use of force and strategy causing much loss of life. In early 1951 he wants to use nuclear weapons against the Chinese or North Koreans, but is relieved of duty by President Truman on April 11, 1951.

1950 THROUGH EARLY 1950s – There were massive UFO sightings. In 1950 there were disc shaped UFOs hovering over the Hanford atomic power plant in Washington State according to one 1970s report found through 'the Freedom of Information Act.' Recent declassified Air Force documents reveal that the U.S. Defense Department has figures showing that from 1952 to 1956 there were 18,662 military aircraft accidents from the Air Force and Navy. Most were explained as training accidents, despite the fact that many of the pilots were expert fliers. The 2007 book, 'Shoot Them Down,' by Frank C. Freshino discusses many specific examples of these UFO/fighter pilot encounters. Freshino discusses some of the events with some of the pilots and military witnesses. MUFON also has much testimony that the Russians were trying to shoot them down for the purpose of back engineering the alien technology. Major Donald Keyhoe confirmed in 1955 through his military sources that Air Force Air Defense Command ordered their pilots to shoot down UFOs.

1950, JANUARY – True magazine publishes an article written by Marine Major Donald Keyhoe called, 'Flying Saucers are Real.' In the article Keyhoe states how the military is covering up the truth about UFOs from the public. The article also pointed toward 'The Extraterrestrial Hypothesis' as a way of explaining the sightings. This hypothesis is the belief that all authentic UFO sightings are of spacecraft traveling from parts of our solar system or Milky Way Galaxy. Major Keyhoe, at that time, worked for the pentagon and eventually became the director of NICAP in 1957. He also wrote popular books on UFOs and did television appearances, such as with Mike Wallace. He was the most significant military witness of his time.

1951, AUGUST 25 – The Lubbock Lights UFO sightings occur and are also witnessed by three science professors/Ph.D.s from Texas Tech University. There were a total of up to 30 lights as bright as stars, but larger in size. Two sets of these lights flew over them and they ruled out meteors as a possible explanation. Against the objections of the professors, the Air Force, under the investigation of Edward Ruppelt, said they were migrating birds.

1951 – Gordan Cooper, astronaut, but then a pilot for the USAF, along with other pilots, fly over Europe and witness an armada of hundreds of flying saucers. They were flying in formation at extremely high altitudes, and at extremely high rates of speed. This was higher and faster than anything that had been developed on earth at the time. The USAF said they were high flying "sea pods." Cooper wrote about this incident and gave testimony on television shows years later.

1951, DECEMBER 20 - The EBR-1 nuclear reactor experimental station opens near Arco, Idaho and generates electricity. It eventually becomes a nuclear power plant.

1952, FEBRUARY 26 – Prime Minister Winston Churchill announces that The United Kingdom has an atomic bomb.

1952, MARCH 22 – Wernher von Braun publishes the first in his series of articles titled, 'Man Will Conquer Space Soon,' including manned flights to Mars and the Moon.

1950 McMinnville, Oregon, Paul Trent Photo

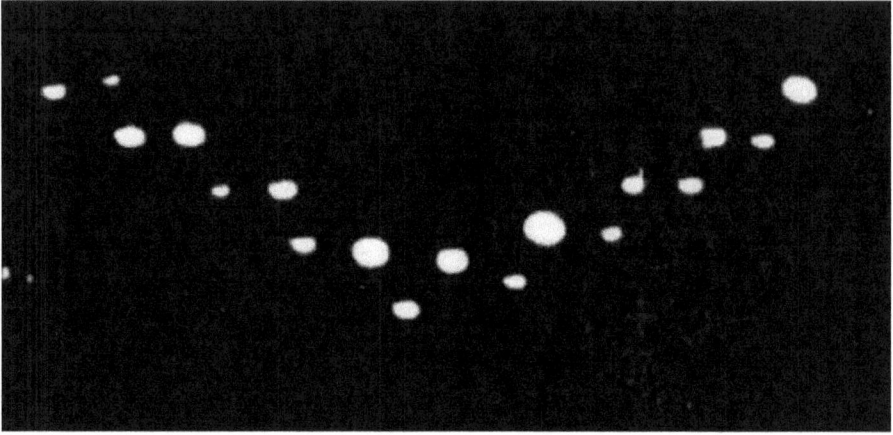

1951 Lubbock, Texas, 'The Lubbock Lights,' Carl Hart Jr.
photo

April 7, 1952 article in Life Magazine

1953 Salem, Massachusetts Coast Guard photo

1952, JULY - Major Donald Keyhoe states, "During the first two weeks of July the saucers reconnaissance of the earth was rapidly stepped up. Over The United States most of the saucers were operating at night, and they seemed to be focusing on defense bases, atomic plants, and military planes." Captain Edward Ruppelt writes in his 1956 book, 'The Report on Unidentified Flying Objects,' "By mid-July we were getting about twenty reports a day plus frantic calls from intelligence officers all over The United States as every Air Force installation in the U.S. was being swamped with reports." In Project Blue Book 1952 had the most unidentified sightings of UFOs. The total sightings were 1,501 in 1952 compared to 12,618 total sighting from 1947 through 1969.

1952 – Felix Bloch and Edward Mills Purcell win the Noble Prize in Physics for work on nuclear magnetic resonance with precision instruments. There has been much speculation about this technology being used in advanced propulsion systems and anti-gravity research.

1952, JULY 14 – A squadron of ten saucer-shaped UFOs is seen by a Pan Am flight over Chesapeake Bay clocked at over 12,000 mph doing impossible maneuvers. There was much media attention over this.

1952, JULY 19 – UFOs fly over Washington D.C. on two consecutive weekends clocked at 7000 mph with extensive radar data and photographs. Truman orders the Air Force to shoot them down, according to multiple major newspaper articles, but they evade and dematerialize on radar according to the thousands of witnesses. Truman must address the mass sightings on national TV and states, "We discuss it at every conference we have with the military (Joints Chiefs of Staff) and they have never been able to make me a concrete report on what they see. There are always things like that going on, flying saucers and we've had other things you know." Some top ranking military officers believed we were being invaded by aliens. The New York Times ran the story on the frontpage, bumping the democratic national convention story. The Air

Force later blames the sightings on "temperature inversions" and the radar data on "false reflections." Kevin D. Randle, Ph.D., Captain, U.S.A.F.R. wrote a book on the subject in 2001 called, 'Invasion Washington, UFOs Over the Capitol.'

1952, JULY 20 – The Washington Post runs the main story on the frontpage, 'Saucer Outran Jet, Pilot Reveals.'

1952, JULY 29 – A press conference at the pentagon presents the military documentation proving the existence of UFOs. It is overseen by General John A. Samford, Air Force Director of Intelligence, who later becomes Director of the NSA in 1956. In the beginning of the televised interview he states how "the recent sightings are not related to any secret development by any agency in The United States and are not a threat to the security of The United States." Major Donald Keyhoe is also interviewed at that time on TV and clearly states, "these sightings are of spacecraft from outer space." At the end of the conference the Air Force does not accept the evidence, but recommends a new Air Force study regarding the phenomenon. The San Francisco Examiner prints the same day, 'The Air Force revealed today that jet pilots have been placed on twenty-four hour nationwide 'alert' against 'flying saucers' with orders to shoot them down if they refuse to land.' Magazine articles about UFOs from publications such as 'Time' and 'Life' create much public interest.

1952 – The Aerial Phenomenon Research Organization (APRO) is created by Jim and Coral Lorenzen. This is a citizen's group.

1952, JULY – Project Blue Book is created under Air Force General Nathan Twining to debunk UFO sightings, replacing Project Grudge. It receives the most UFO reports in its seventeen year history for the months of June and July, totaling 648. This included 235 USAF fighters involved in major accidents with 94 fighter aircraft destroyed and 51 fatalities.

Washington, D. C. 1952, Capitol

1952 Photo of UFOs flying over the Capitol

CAA Radar Man Tracks Flying Saucers Over Washington, Can't Explain Them

By HARRY G. BARNES
Written for NEA Service

WASHINGTON — Shortly after midnight on July 19, Ed Nugent pulled me over to the radar scope and laughingly said:

"Here's a fleet of flying saucers for you."

As it turns out now, Ed could very well have been stating an absolute fact.

I am a senior air route traffic controller for the Civil Aeronautics Administration and was in charge of the air route traffic control center that particular night at National Airport. Briefly, part of our job is to constantly monitor the skies around the nation's capital with the electronic eye of radar for purposes of controlling air traffic.

Our shift had come on duty 45 minutes earlier. Eight men were

1952, July 31 in 'The Daily Star,' Sudbury, Ontario

62

Fall River (MA) *Herald-News*, July 29, 1952

Jets Told to Shoot Down Flying Discs

Air Force Puzzled But No Longer Skeptical

By DARRELL GARWOOD

WASHINGTON, (INS)—The Air Force, stumped by the inability of 600-mile-an-hour jet planes to catch "flying saucers," turned today to a new type camera to solve the 5-year-old sky mystery.

Jet pilots are operating under a 24-hour nation-wide "alert" to chase the mysterious objects and to "shoot them down" if they ignore orders to land.

However, the Air Force confessed that none of its jets have come within shooting range of the blinking, enigmatic flying discs.

Several pilots, according to the Air Force, have tried to shoot down the mysterious discs but the "steady bright lights" in the sky have outflown the pilots by as much as a thousand miles an hour.

An AF spokesman said a new-type camera may be able to bring the mystery to an end. He said the camera photographs "luminous phenomenon." It uses the principle employed by astronomers in determining the composition of stars. Air Force scientists hope to determine the physical makeup of the phenomenon and identify its source.

Maj. Gen. John A. Samford, chief of Air Force Intelligence, said the new type cameras have been ordered and will be distributed to jet plane pilots as soon as they become available.

Meanwhile, as new reports continued to pour into the Pentagon of more sightings of mysterious objects the Air Force summoned several "saucer" specialists from Dayton, Ohio, for a conference today.

Called to Washington were Capt. E. J. Ruppelt and several fellow officers from the Air Technical Intelligence Center at Wright-Patterson Field.

The Air Force said it is receiving new reports of "flying saucers" at the rate of 100 a month.

The Air Force contended that its intensive investigation of more than 1,000 "saucer" reports has convinced it that they are not being sent over the United States by an enemy.

The AF added that its investigation indicated also that they are not being controlled by "a reasoning body."

Forty-eight hours of intensive investigation has failed to explain radar and visual observation of unidentified objects accompanied by brilliant white and colored lights on two successive weekends over Washington. The so-called "saucers" were seen on both Air Force and Civil Aeronautic Authority radarscopes. How the CAA sightings were made was described by a radar specialist, James M. Ritchay of the Washington Air Route Traffic Control Center.

"Dozen Objects"

Until unidentified objects began moving onto our radarscopes, I thought people who reported flying saucers were just seeing things," he said.

"Now I don't know what to think. I have talked to representatives of the Air Force, and they say they can't explain the appearance of the flying objects.

"All we can do is tell you what we saw on our instruments, and

(Continued on Page Six)

(From Barry Greenwood newsclipping collection)

The Washington Post — FINAL

'Saucer' Outran Jet, Pilot Reveals

U. S. Protests Soviet 'Hate' In Aviation Day Posters

Russians Rule Satellites By Torture and Murder

Stevenson And Truman Head 'Big 3' Campaign

Eisenhower, Nixon Plan Campaign

Investigation On in Secret After Chase Over Capital

1952, JULY – The Roberson Panel (CIA run according to Donald Keyhoe) is created to reduce interest in UFOs among the public and begin monitoring civilian UFO groups, such as APRO. Carl Sagan and Thornton Page were members of the panel. The panel was first to employ the 'ridicule the witness' strategy. This was Truman's attempt at silencing what had become 'the UFO Party' within the military and civilian sector. Dewey Fournet, Edward Ruppelt and a few higher ups were on the military side. Donald Keyhoe, Frank Edwards and other UFO civilian organizations were on the civilian side.

1952, JULY 28 – The Fall River Herald Newspaper of Massachusetts runs a story, 'Jets told to Shoot Down Flying Saucers – Air Force Puzzled but no Longer Skeptical.'

1952, JULY 29 – The Seattle Post Intelligencer carried an International News Service story with the headlines, 'Air Force Orders Jet Pilots to Shoot Down Flying Saucers if They Refuse to Land.'

1952, SEPTEMBER 6 – Flatwoods Monster sighting occurs in Braxton County, West Virginia. There were six craft sighted, two of which crashed, with a third blowing up. Reptilian like humanoids were seen hovering around the ships according to witnesses. The U.S. Air Force and National Guard take over within hours of the incident and create the cover story that it was a meteorite sighting.

1952, OCTOBER 3 – Great Britain detonates its first nuclear bomb in Australia.

Left to right: R. L. Jones, Roger Ramey, Edward Ruppelt, John Samford, Donald Bower

Dr. J. Allen Hynek

Major Donald Keyhoe

Dr. Howard P. Robertson

SCIENTIFIC ADVISORY PANEL ON
UNIDENTIFIED FLYING OBJECTS
14 - 17 January 1953

MEMBERS	ORGANIZATION	FIELD OF COMPETENCY
Dr. H. P. Robertson (Chairman)	California Institute of Technology	Physics, weapons systems
Dr. Luis W. Alvarez	University of California	Physics, radar
Dr. Lloyd V. Berkner	Associated Universities, Inc.	Geophysics
Dr. Samuel Goudsmit	Brookhaven National Laboratories	Atomic structure, statistical problems
Dr. Thornton Page	Office of Research Operations, Johns Hopkins University	Astronomy, Astrophysics
ASSOCIATE MEMBERS		
Dr. J. Allen Hynek	Ohio State University	Astronomy
Mr. Frederick C. Durant	Arthur D. Little, Inc.	Rockets, guided missiles
INTERVIEWEES		
Brig. Gen. William M. Garland	Commanding General, ATIC	Scientific and technical intelligence
Dr. H. Marshall Chadwell	Assistant Director, O/SI, CIA	Scientific and technical intelligence
Mr. Ralph L. Clark	Deputy Assistant Director, O/SI, CIA	Scientific and technical intelligence

Declassified by ___006687___
Date ___2 8 MAR 1975___

70

Witness rendition of 'The Flatwoods Monster'

CENTRAL INTELLIGENCE AGENCY
WASHINGTON 25, D. C.

OFFICE OF THE DIRECTOR

008014

MEMORANDUM TO: Director, Psychological Strategy Board

SUBJECT: Flying Saucers

1. I am today transmitting to the National Security Council a proposal (TAB A) in which it is concluded that the problems connected with unidentified flying objects appear to have implications for psychological warfare as well as for intelligence and operations.

2. The background for this view is presented in some detail in TAB B.

3. I suggest that we discuss at an early board meeting the possible offensive or defensive utilization of these phenomena for psychological warfare purposes.

Walter B. Smith
Director

Enclosure

RELEASED 5/9/94

- 52 -

Walter B. Smith was the fourth Director of the CIA
from October 1950 to February 1953

72

1952, OCTOBER 24 – The National Security Agency, NSA, is formally established by Truman in a classified memorandum. The public did not know of its existence at that time. It reports to the Department of Defense and is an intelligence agency responsible for global monitoring and counter surveillance. They are the first to receive any images from space. In 1966 they reviewed images from the five lunar orbiters before briefing NASA.

1952, OCTOBER 31 – The United States detonates a significant 10.4 megaton nuclear device at Eniwetok, Marshall Islands called Ivy Mike.

1952, NOVEMBER 1 – The first hydrogen bomb is detonated in the Marshall Islands, and underground test detonations occur in Nevada in early 1952, eight total. This gave The United States a short-lived advantage in the nuclear arms race with The Soviet Union.

1953, JANUARY 20 – Dwight D. Eisenhower becomes the 34th president of The United States.

1953, JANUARY – 4602 Air Intelligence Service Squad (AISS) was created by General Woodbury M. Burgess for the Air Force. This was a more specific international UFO retrieval team reporting to Air Material Command, later called the Air Tactical Intelligence Center (ATIC), in Dayton, Ohio. They had special names for their operations, such as 'Operation Blue Fly' and later in 1957 'Project Moondust.'

1953, JANUARY – The Pentacle Memorandum is written and distributed to classified internal UFO researchers, such as Dr. Allen Hynek. This document discussed the MJ-12 group's research and proved their existence. Researcher Jacques Vallee saw this document years later when working with Hynek.

1953, MAY 20 – Kingman, Arizona UFO crash occurs and a retrieval team takes the 30 foot flying saucer and dead alien bodies to Wright-Patterson AFB.

1953 – General Benjamin Chidlaw, former Commander General of Air Defense Command states in an interview, "We have a stack of reports of flying saucers. We take them seriously, when you consider we have lost many men and planes trying to intercept them."

1953, SEPTEMBER – The International Flying Saucers Bureau is dissolved by its founder, Albert K. Bender, after his claims of being threatened by 'men in black.' This was an UFO citizen group founded in 1952 with publications in 48 states. They published quarterly articles, some in 'Space Review,' the official UFO magazine at that time. Some researchers have accused Bender of being an hoaxter.

1953, NOVEMBER 20 – Scott Crossfield becomes the first pilot to fly twice the speed of sound, 1291 miles per hour/Mach 2.005, at Muroc AFB.

1953, DECEMBER – The Joint Chiefs of Staff issued Army-Navy-Air Force publication 146 that made the unauthorized release of information concerning UFOs a crime under the Espionage Act. It was punishable by up to ten years in prison and a $10,000 fine.

1954, FEBRUARY 15 – Journalist Dorothy Kilgallen writes in 'The New York Evening Journal,' "Flying saucers are regarded as of such vital importance that they will be the subject of a special hush-hush meeting of the world military heads next summer."

1954, FEBRUARY 20 – Eisenhower is to have met with extraterrestrials, the Nordics, at Edwards AFB, then called Muroc. His great granddaughter, Laura Magdalene Eisenhower, claims that the family knew of this meeting. The first reports shared by some of the attendees at the meeting discuss President Eisenhower being offered a diplomatic exchange of peaceful technology with an educational/spiritual program making the people of earth aware of their presence. In exchange, people of the earth would end the nuclear weapons program. It was said that Eisenhower rejected the offer and stated that the people of earth were not ready for disclosure. It was also stated that Eisenhower was angered when the extraterrestrials stated that they would continue to make isolated contact with certain people, and then dematerialized. There has been much misinformation published about this meeting. There have been other reports of additional meetings with other alien races, such as the Greys, and possible treaties signed. This is unlikely since the U.S. Air Force and Navy continued to fire upon UFOs through the 1950s and ramped up nuclear bomb testing. Famous radio commentator Frank Edwards promptly broke this story and presented it as discussed above based on varied reports he received. Edwards was then a household name in the radio world on the Mutual Broadcasting System as host to nationwide news and opinion. He was fired a short time later in 1954, never to return to this prominent radio station because of his discussions of UFOs. There were thousands of letters protesting his dismissal.

1954, FEBRUARY 28 – The largest U.S. test detonation occurs with a 15 megaton yield at Bikini Atoll, Marshal Islands. It is called Castle Bravo and caused the greatest amount of radiation damage of any nuclear testing event in U.S. history. It was 1000 times more powerful than the bomb dropped on Hiroshima.

1954, MARCH - Civilian Saucer Intelligence of New York is a newly formed civilian UFO organization. They introduced UFO research books from France.

1954, MARCH 10 – The Joint Chiefs of Staff implement JANAP 146 (C), which establishes UFO reporting instructions for all military personnel. Along with part 'B,' it prohibits making any public statements about UFOs.

1954, MARCH 26 – The United States detonates another significant nuclear device at Bikini Atoll called Castle Romeo. It had an eleven megaton yield.

1954, APRIL – Eisenhower has the secret service adopt a secret policy stating that all information related to UFOs is a matter of national security and is classified. It is written in internal documents that "under no circumstances is the public or press to know of the existence of extraterrestrials. The official government policy is that extraterrestrials do not exist."

1954, APRIL – MJ-12 creates an operation manual called 'SOM1-01' for protocols involving recovering UFOs. It gives extensive instructions on how to deal with the public to maintain secrecy and debunk witness testimony. These protocols are still used today. The manual reads: "For Majestic Eyes Only."

1954, MAY 29 – The Bilderberg Group holds their first meeting at the Bilderberg Hotel in Oosterbeek, Netherlands. It is co-funded by the CIA, and the CIA co-funded other early Bilderberg Group meetings. This is comprised of the most powerful and wealthy people in The United States and Europe. One of the founders, Prince Bernard of the Netherlands, contacted the former U.S. CIA Director, Walter Bedell Smith, directly and asked for his attendance. Smith was well informed of all UFO activity in The United States. Every year at their annual meeting about 80 visitors are invited to present their ideas to the members. Roughly two thirds of its approximate 140 members are from Europe and one third are from The United States. They control the banking, energy, and media industries, as well as the then newly formed military industrial complex. The Dulles brothers were regular participants. The American Rockefeller family, Great Britain's Rothschild family, and other European royalty are prominent members. Some of the current participants or members include George Soros (their most public member), the Clintons, George Bush Sr., Mitt Romney, Warren Buffet, Henry Kissinger, David Patraeus, Timothy Geithner, Michael Bloomberg, Lindsey Graham, and John Kerry. Much of the group's background can be found in Daniel Estulin's 2005 book, 'The True Story of the Bilderberg Group.' In American politics these are the people referred to as "the establishment or globalist elites" found in both the democrat and republican parties.

FROM WHENCE IT GOT ITS NAME: Above is a photo of the Hotel de Bilderberg, the hotel that hosted the first Bilderberg meeting all the way back in 1954. Bilderberg meetings have been held every year since then, with the venue sites getting more lavish every year. Bilderberg has at times taken to meeting on islands, ostensibly because it's easier to keep reporters and photographers away so no one can document those participants who attend.

The Prince presides at the First Bilderberg Conference, Oosterbeek, 1954

DAY TWO of a dossier on the quiet men who control our destiny

THE Daily Mirror yesterday revealed the power of the Trilateral Commission as a group of global manipulators. The Trilateral Commission—known as the Kingmakers—stands second to none in power, prestige and influence. But not far behind comes the Bilderberg Group, a circle of the elite and wealthy whose hush-hush meetings determine how the Western nations should run their affairs.

SECRET MEETINGS TO SHAPE THE WORLD

by ROBERT ERINGER

An American journalist who has spent four years investigating the all-powerful groups that aim to influence our lives.

EVERY year 120 of the world's most powerful and influential men come together, lock themselves away for three days and decide what policies the democratic nations of the West should follow.

They are members of the Bilderberg Group and their meetings are always kept a closely guarded secret.

But I can reveal that this year they will meet in the spa city of Aachen, just 45 miles from the German capital, Bonn, from April 18 - 20 inclusive.

I can also reveal that former German President Walter Scheel has been invited to replace the ageing Lord Home as chairman of Bilderberg. Scheel has accepted.

Top of the Aachen agenda will be world politics and economics following the Russian invasion of Afghanistan.

Bilderbergers represent the elite and wealthy establishment of every Western nation. They include bankers, politicians, diplomats and leaders of the giant multi-national corporations.

Among British politicians who have attended their meetings are Edward Heath, Harold Wilson, James Callaghan, Denis Healey, Margaret Thatcher and Enoch Powell.

Other influential members of the British Establishment include Lord Roll, of merchant bankers S. G. Warburg; Sir Reay Geddes, chairman of Dunlop; John Harvey-Jones of ICI; and Sir David Steel, chairman of British Petroleum.

Everything about the group is shrouded in mystery.

Their meetings, which take place at a different location each year, go unannounced, their debates unreported, their decisions unknown.

Trace

Ideas and suggestions made at Bilderberg.

C. Gordon Tether, the distinguished former columnist of the Financial Times, wrote: "If the Bilderberg Group is not a conspiracy of some sort it is conducted in such a way as to give a remarkably good imitation of one."

Walter Bedell Smith, then director of the CIA.

One of the most intriguing aspects of the Bilderberg group is its steering committee's amazing ability to invite politicians to join the group who later reach the pinnacles of power in their respective countries.

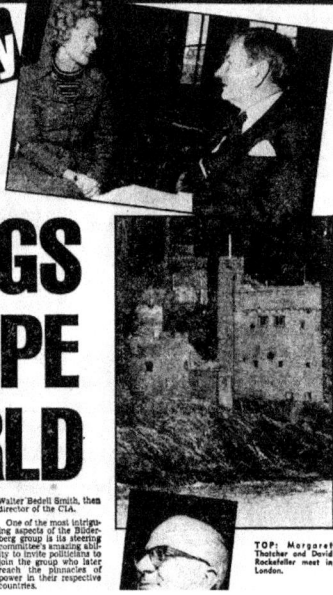

TOP: Margaret Thatcher and David Rockefeller meet in London.

1980, February 13th, 'The Daily Mirror'

David Rockefeller with Margaret Thatcher

1954, JUNE 27 – The world's first nuclear power plant generates enough power for a power grid in Obninsk, Soviet Union.

1954, AUGUST 12 - Air Force Regulation AFR 200-2 is established by order of Nathan F. Twining, Chief of Staff, USAF. This forbids all military personnel to make any public statements about UFOs.

1954, AUGUST 30 – The Atomic Energy Act of 1954 is signed by Eisenhower. This encouraged private corporations to build nuclear reactors and allowed them to obtain restricted technical data for nuclear energy production. In the first years there were many partial core meltdowns and accidents, but these reports were kept from the public.

1954, DECEMBER – Ben Rich, propulsion systems program manager, aerospace engineer, and future CEO of Lockheed in 1975 is transferred to Skunk Works. He would become the creator of the F117 Stealth Fighter.

1955 – General Douglas MacArthur gives a West Point graduation speech and says, "The nations of the world will have to unite, for the next war will be an interplanetary war. The nations of the earth must someday make a common front against attack by people of other planets." Clearly the general had a firm belief in extraterrestrials.

1955, FEBRUARY 2 – William Lear, creator of the Lear jet, gives a press conference in Bogota, Columbia. He states, "flying saucers come from outer space and are piloted by beings of superior intelligence." On February tenth in Grand Rapids, Michigan he tells reporters that he had seen an UFO himself and that an American aviation company was conducting gravitational-field research. In a November 1955 article in the 'New York Herald-Tribune' he is quoted as having his company researching artificial electo-gravitational fields.

1955, MAY 23 – Dorothy Kilgallen, outspoken journalist, writes an article in the L.A. Times about how the British had examined debris from a crashed flying saucer with dead aliens and determined it had originated from another planet.

1955 – The CIA has Lockheed aerospace engineer Kelly Johnson start construction of area 51, originally called Groom Lake. It is a remote detachment of Edwards AFB.

1955, NOVEMBER 20 – The New York Herald-Tribune publishes an article, 'Conquest of Gravity Top Aim of Top Scientists in U.S.' It explained how private corporations, such as General Dynamics and Martin Aircraft, have been working diligently on anti-gravity technology. It also explained how some universities, such as Princeton, Purdue, and Indiana, have been doing research in this area.

1955 – The Miami Herald publishes a three part series on 1950s gravity research. It names Princeton, Purdue, University of Indiana, MIT, and University of North Carolina as research centers. It states that most of America's major aircraft firms were involved with gravity research, including Martin, Convair, Bell Aircraft, Lear, Clarke Electronics, and Sperry-Rand Corporation. It said this research may provide unlimited energy for mankind and provide propulsion systems eliminating 'G' forces, while providing much faster acceleration.

1956, FEBRUARY 1 – The Army Ballistic Missile Agency (ABMA) is formed to develop the U.S. Army's first large ballistic missile at Redstone Arsenal. It is headed by Wernher von Braun as technical director and is commanded by Major General John B. Medaris. This is where the Redstone Missile was developed as a direct descendent of the V-2 German missile. ABMA developed the three-stage-rocket and large booster program. ABMA was considered 'the working group on vehicular program.'

1956, MAY 6 – A semi-documentary major movie comes out called, 'UFOS, The True Story of Flying Saucers.' This was written by Al Chop, ex-marine and press reporter liaison to the pentagon during its investigation of UFOs from 1947 to 1950. The film shows the actual, military verified, classified film footage and evidence. It includes the reenactment of the radar situation room when flying saucers flew over the Capitol in 1952. The film was distributed by United Artists and can be seen today.

1956, AUGUST 29 – The National Investigation Committee on Aerial Phenomenon (NICAP) is founded in Washington D.C. by Townsend Brown with the aim of ending UFO secrecy. It was also the main civilian organization for collecting UFO sightings, and they had extensive records, some with radar documentation. Brown was a researcher of electromagnetism and gravity fields. He did not run the organization well financially so Donald Keyhoe took over as director in 1957. They were able to recruit many high ranking military members, including Vice Admiral Roscoe Hilenkoetter, first director of the CIA. Civilian members included Frank Edwards, Leonard Stringfield, and many from academia. The board of governors was very stable for most of the organization's existence. By 1958 they had 5000 members. The CIA infiltrated NICAP in the late 1960s and early 1970s to discredit and shut down this highly credible organization.

1956 – Kelly Johnson becomes VP of R&D/Chief Engineer at Lockheed. He developed the Lockheed U2 spy aircraft in the early 1950s.

1956, OCTOBER 17 – The world's first full scale nuclear power station is open at Calder Hall, Great Britain.

1957 – A spike in total UFO sightings occur in 1957 as recorded in Project Blue Book. There were 1006 sightings, up from 670 the year before and 627 the year after.

1957, MAY 3 – Astronaut Gordon Cooper, then a test pilot, witnesses and films an UFO saucer land at Edwards AFB. A colonel at the base orders him not to copy the film and send it to

Washington D.C. The film is never heard of again and Washington denies its existence.

1957, JULY 12 – A letter is written to General Twining from ATIC, Advanced Technical Intelligence Center, Wright-Patterson AFB, admitting that pilots are firing on UFOs. It is signed by Wallace Elwood. Additional specific names and dates verifying this can be found in Major Donald Keyhoe's 1973 book, 'Aliens from Space: The Real Story of Unidentified Flying Objects.'

1957, AUGUST – North American Aerospace Defense Command (NORAD) announces its formation and approval by the Joint Chiefs of Staff. It provides aerospace warning and air surveillance for the defense of North America. It is based at Wright-Patterson AFB, Dayton, Ohio, but has facilities at Elmendorf AFB, Alaska and at the Cheyenne Mountain bunker in Colorado Springs, Colorado. The bunker was built in 1961.

1957 Fort Belvoir, Virginia

1957 Edwards AFB, Southern California

Holloman A F B 1957

1957 Holloman AFB, Otero County, New Mexico

I know other astronauts share my feelings.... And we know the government is sitting on hard evidence of UFOs.

— Gordon Cooper —

AZ QUOTES

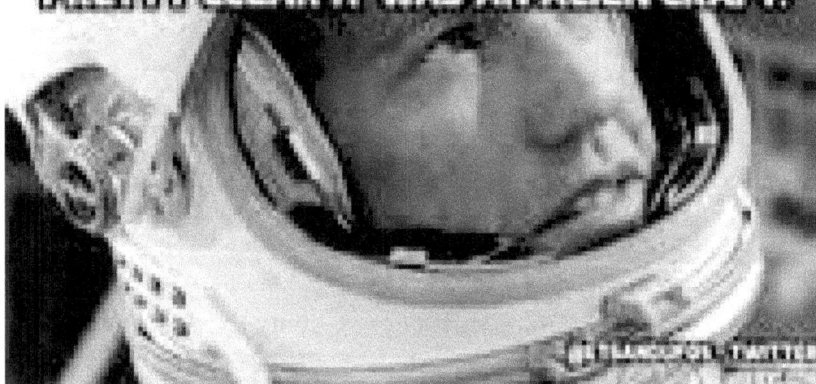

"I HAD A CAMERA CREW FILMING THE INSTALLATION WHEN THEY SPOTTED A SAUCER. THEY FILMED IT AS IT FLEW OVERHEAD, THEN HOVERED, EXTENDED THREE LEGS AS LANDING GEAR AND SLOWLY CAME DOWN TO LAND ON A DRY LAKE BED. IT WAS A CLASSIC SAUCER, SHINY SILVER AND SMOOTH, ABOUT 30 FEET ACROSS. IT WAS PRETTY CLEAR IT WAS AN ALIEN CRAFT."

1957, OCTOBER 4 – Sputnik 1 is launched from The Soviet Union and becomes the first artificial satellite in space.

1958, JANUARY 1 – Explorer 1 becomes the first U.S. satellite launched into space.

1958, FEBRUARY – Advanced Research Projects Agency (ARPA) is created by the Eisenhower administration and reports to senior Department of Defense. Its mission is to ensure that the U.S. military technology is more sophisticated and advanced than its enemies. This was in direct response to The Soviet Union's launching of Sputnik into space on October 4th, 1957. The space research portion is soon transferred to NASA and the future NRO. It is renamed DARPA in March of 1972. This is the government organization now developing genetically enhanced soldiers, as well as other advanced technologies.

1958, MARCH - The Army Ordinance Missile Command is created to control the Army Ballistic Agency, the Redstone Arsenal, the Jet Propulsion Laboratory, White Sands Proving Ground, and the Army Rocket and Guided Missile Agency. This was commanded by Major General John B. Medaris.

1958, JULY 29 – The National Aeronautics and Space Administration (NASA) is created by the Eisenhower administration as a non-military public entity. It is in charge of the nation's civilian aerospace program and civilian aerospace research. This was created by a transformation of the Army Ordinance Missile Command and the National Advisory Committee for Aeronautics. NASA then formed the George C. Marshall Space Flight Center, headed by Wernher von Braun.

1958 SEPREMBER 12 – The integrated circuit was first demonstrated with a working example. This is commonly known as the computer chip.

1958, DECEMBER 22 – 450 airline pilots sign a petition and present it to congress protesting the official policy of debunking UFO sightings. Under JANAP 146 they faced up to ten years in jail if they revealed details of their sightings to the media. This report fell on deaf ears and was swept away by the Air Force.

WASH. POST. 30 JULY 1958

Flying Objects Real, Psychiatrist Insists

ALAMOGORDO, N. M., July 29 (UPI)—Dr. Carl Jung, the father of analytical psychology, said today that so-called unidentified flying objects "are not mere rumor" and the U. S. Air Force was "creating panic" by withholding information about them.

Jung's statements were printed in the monthly bulletin of the Aerial Phenomena Research Organization, UFO filter center. Jung serves as chief psychologist for the center.

"In the course of years, I gathered a considerable mass of observations," Jung wrote. "However, I can only say for certain these things are not mere rumor. Something has been seen.

"A purely sychological explanation is ruled out by the

Associated Press Photo

DR. CARL JUNG

"... something has been seen"

1959, APRIL 20 – Astronomer/author Morris K. Jessup was found dead from exhaust pipe asphyxiation in his car. His book, 'The Case for the UFO' had most proof sources for UFOs from the 1800s. He later suggested a fantastic conspiracy involving government cover-ups and advanced physical experimentation. He speculated about anti-gravitational propulsion systems and electromagnetism, as well as the Philadelphia Experiment dealing with space and time. Jessup was a friend of UFO researcher Ivan Sanderson, who also died under questionable circumstances.

1959, DECEMBER 24 – Inspector General of the Air Force issued a warning to all air base commanders in the continental U.S.: "Unidentified flying objects – sometimes treated lightly by the press and referred to as flying saucers – must be rapidly and accurately identified as serious USAF business in the Interior Zone. Technical and defense considerations will continue to exist in this area."

1960 – Project Ozma in West Virginia, under Frank Drake, now director of SETI, uses a giant dish to listen for space noise. According to Donald Keyhoe in his 1973 book, 'Aliens from Space: The Real Story of Unidentified Flying Objects,' within two minutes of being turned on there was a strong signal coming from Tau Ceti that was unmistakable intelligent code. Carl Sagan was among the many attendees. The Air Force shuts it down immediately under the direction of Dr. Otto Struve, renowned astronomer. Frank Edwards also wrote of this event and it was suggested that the project did not die, but moved to Arecibo, Puerto Rico.

1960, FEBRUARY 28 – Admiral Roscoe Hillenkoetter, first director of the CIA and member of MJ-12, writes and article in the New York Times titled, 'Air Force Order on "Flying Saucer" Cited.' He declares it is time for public disclosure and calls for congressional hearings because this is "serious business." The CIA and Air Force pressured Hillenkoetter , as with Ruppelt, to change his position on the subject and resign from NICAP.

1960, AUGUST 25 – The National Reconnaissance Office (NRO) is created by Eisenhower and his staff to coordinate spy activities between the CIA and Air Force, and eventually the Navy and the NSA. They conduct intelligence related activities for U.S. security with the main focus being spy satellites, all of which is classified. The public and most of the congress did not know of their existence until 1973. Based on their enormous annual budget some researchers, such as Stanton Friedman, have speculated that this may be one of the main organizations from which experimental spacecraft come. They were the first ones to screen pictures taken in space and censor them. This is the organization that air brushes out anomalies on the moon pictures and created a seven second delay of transmissions from space to censor pictures or astronaut live reports.

1960, SEPTEMBER 15 – Air Force Captain Edward Ruppelt, aerospace engineer, UFO author, head of Project Grudge from 1951 to 1953, dies of an heart attack at age 37. He criticized the Air Force for not being objective, admitted that there was a cover-up to his military friends, worked with NICAP for disclosure, and pushed for public hearings with congress. He also published, 'The Report on Unidentified Flying Objects' in 1955, which documented many UFO cases and supported disclosure. In the spring of 1959 there were three new chapters added to the book debunking the UFO phenomenon. Ruppelt was under extreme pressure by the Air Force to change his views on the topic.

1961, JANUARY 17 – President Eisenhower gives his televised farewell speech and warns about 'the military-industrial complex.' He realized by then that he had lost control of the UFO information.

1961, JANUARY 20 – John Fitzgerald Kennedy takes office as the 35th President of the United States.

1961, APRIL 12 – Yuri Gagarin becomes the first astronaut to travel to space aboard the Russian Vostok 3KA-3 (Vostok 1).

1961, MAY 5 – Alan Shepard becomes the first American Astronaut to travel to space from Florida aboard the Freedom 7 spacecraft.

1961, SEPTEMBER 19 – Betty and Barney Hill are abducted by an UFO in New Hampshire. This is the first publicized abduction case in The United States. An increase of reports of the abduction phenomenon start to occur and continue.

First documented American UFO abductees

Betty and Barney Hill

1961, OCTOBER 1 – The Defense Intelligence Agency (DIA) is created by the Kennedy administration under the Department of Defense. They are the main foreign military espionage organization.

1961, OCTOBER 30 - The Soviet Union detonates the largest nuclear device ever tested called Tsar Bomba, test #130. It had a 50 megaton yield and was tested at Novaya Zemlya.

1962, APRIL 18 – The Las Vegas UFO crash occurs near Nellis AFB. Over 1000 people witnessed it moving across the states. It was cigar shaped and "looked like a red, exploding sword." Fighter jets were scrambled and there was radar documentation. The Air force claimed it was a bolide, but researcher Kevin Randle concluded that it was an extraterrestrial craft after his lengthy investigation. He explains the crash details in his 1995 book, 'A History of UFO Crashes.' There were nuclear missiles stored at Nellis AFB.

BRILLIANT RED EXPLOSION FLARES IN LAS VEGAS SKY

Las Vegas ⊙ SUN

Trucks Hauling TNT Seen as LV Hazard

1962, AUGUST 3 – Marilyn Monroe, actress and model, dies at age 36 from an apparent suicide. FBI and CIA documents indicate that she was threatening to have a news conference and tell all about her involvement with the Kennedy brothers and UFO secrecy. She was very disgruntled about the Kennedy's ignoring her. There were rumors that she had learned about the UFO secrecy from secret lover JFK.

1962, APRIL 25 THROUGH OCTOBER 30 - Operation Dominic occurs around the Hawaiian Islands at high altitude. There were 31 nuclear test explosions during the 'Bay of Pigs' event in response to the Soviet's resumption of nuclear testing after a tacit 1958-1961 test moratorium. UFOs were spotted by the Navy during the tests and the Navy gave pursuit, according to one of the Richard Dolan UFO investigations.

1962, NOVEMBER 4 – The last Pacific Proving Ground detonation occurs.

1962 – John Glenn becomes the first American to orbit around the earth and reports seeing orbs during space flight. NASA called them "fire flies."

1963, FEBRUARY 11 – The CIA established a domestic operations division for its clandestine services, one of which was MK-Search. Many investigations dealt with ways to destabilize human personalities. This was at a time when the NSA's 'Operation Shamrock' flourished with new found technology in RCA's global development of computerized magnetic tape. The NSA started 'watch lists' of names and organizations, spying on everyone by looking for key words and phrases.

1963, JUNE 10 – JFK gives his 'peace speech' at the commencement ceremony for American University outlining the need for peace with Russia.

1963, NOVEMBER 11 – The Russian Cosmos 21 space launch fails in space under mysterious circumstances. It is speculated by some researchers that UFOs interfered with some of the Russian missile launches because of Russia's past aggressiveness in trying to shoot UFOs down for reverse engineering purposes.

1963, NOVEMBER 12 – Kennedy writes a national security memorandum to NASA instructing them to work with the Soviet space program. He orders the CIA, via memo, to share U.S. secrets about UFOs with the Russians. Kennedy is also concerned that UFO sightings by either side may spark a nuclear war.

1963, NOVEMBER 22 – President Kennedy is assassinated and no one works with the Soviets. Vice President Lyndon B. Johnson becomes the 36th President of the United States.

1963, DECEMBER 22 – Truman writes in 'The Washington Post,' "he is disturbed by the way in which the CIA has been diverted from its original assignment. It has become a government all of its own and all secret. They don't have to account to anybody." President Kennedy had made statements to this effect before his death, but also mentioned that they do not have the best interests of America or the American people in mind. Kennedy wanted to dismantle the CIA and stated that they were only protecting the interests of "the establishment or status quo." I remember seeing video clips of JFK saying this on television when I was a boy.

THE WHITE HOUSE
WASHINGTON

November 12, 1963

NATIONAL SECURITY ACTION MEMORANDUM NO. 271

MEMORANDUM FOR

The Administrator, National Aeronautics and Space
Administration

SUBJECT: Cooperation with the USSR on Outer Space Matters

I would like you to assume personally the initiative and central
responsibility within the Government for the development of a
program of substantive cooperation with the Soviet Union in the
field of outer space, including the development of specific technical proposals. I assume that you will work closely with the
Department of State and other agencies as appropriate.

These proposals should be developed with a view to their possible discussion with the Soviet Union as a direct outcome of
my September 20 proposal for broader cooperation between
the United States and the USSR in outer space, including cooperation in lunar landing programs. All proposals or suggestions originating within the Government relating to this
general subject will be referred to you for your consideration
and evaluation.

In addition to developing substantive proposals, I expect that
you will assist the Secretary of State in exploring problems of
procedure and timing connected with holding discussions with
the Soviet Union and in proposing for my consideration the
channels which would be most desirable from our point of
view. In this connection the channel of contact developed

SecDef Control No. X7448

JFK asking for cooperation with the USSR on outer space
matters

November 12, 1963

MEMORANDUM FOR
The Director,   Central Intelligence Agency

SUBJECT: Classification Review of all UFO Intelligence Files Affecting
National Security

As I had discussed with you previously, I have initiated   and
have instructed James Webb to develop a program with the Soviet Union in
joint space and lunar exploration. It would be very helpful if you would have
furnished Soviet codes devised with the purpose of penetralization of known flying
as allowed for classified CIA and USAF sources. It is important that we
have a clear distinction between the known and unknown in the event the
surprise may be mislaid our enemies comprehension as a cover for intelligence
gathering of both defense and space programs.

When this data has been worked out, I would like you to arrange a program
of data sharing with NASA where Unknowns are a factor. This will help NASA
mission directors in their defensive   .

I would like an interim report on the data review as soon as this February 1,
1964.

                    For John F. Kennedy

JFK asking the CIA to share all UFO intelligence with the
Soviets

1963 – Anti-gravity, or 'G-projects,' were suppressed in the scientific community, as explained in Nick Cook's 2001 book, 'The Hunt for Zero Point.' There was much speculation that anti-gravity technology was related to free energy. Discussion of the subject was then considered taboo among physicists. According to one retired aerospace engineer I interviewed the government went to all universities and certain companies working on G-projects to seize their work in the early 1960s.

1964 – NATO writes a report called, 'An Assessment' to explain the many radar UFO sightings in Europe. This was reported to Army General Lyman L. Lemnitzer, Supreme Allied Commander of NATO. It was decided that humanity was not ready for disclosure. The UFO phenomenon was then reclassified as 'cosmic top secret' according to retired U.S. Army Command Sergeant Major Robert Dean.

1964 – USAF First Lieutenant Robert Jacobs, Ph.D. films an UFO shutting down an Atlas Missile during test flight. This happened at Vandenberg AFB in California. Jacobs was told not to speak of the incident by the CIA and the film was confiscated. Jacobs has testified to this event on camera and at disclosure events.

1964, DECEMBER 10 – Fort Riley Army Base in Kansas recovers nine alien bodies in a nearby UFO crash.

1965 – 46 antigravity, 'G-projects' were confirmed to Major Donald Keyhoe by the Scientific Information Exchange of the Smithsonian Institute. 33 of the projects were Air Force controlled. Among the companies involved were Bell Labs, Boeing, Convair, Douglas, Hughs, Lockheed, and Martin.

1965 TO MID 1970S – Dozens of UFO encounters occur at all US military bases housing nuclear weapons. It was reported by 1975 that UFOs changed targeting codes at some bases, shut down missile silos, disabled flying rockets, and altered the flight paths of some rockets shot into space. This continues today in all countries that have nuclear weapons. Richard Dolan explains some of these encounters in his 2002 book, 'UFOs and the National Security State.'

1965, JUNE 4 – Astronaut James McDivitt reports seeing an UFO while on the Gemini 4 mission. Astronaut Frank Borman later that year reports seeing an UFO while on the Gemini 7 mission. Critics in the Condon Committee could not easily explain these sightings away.

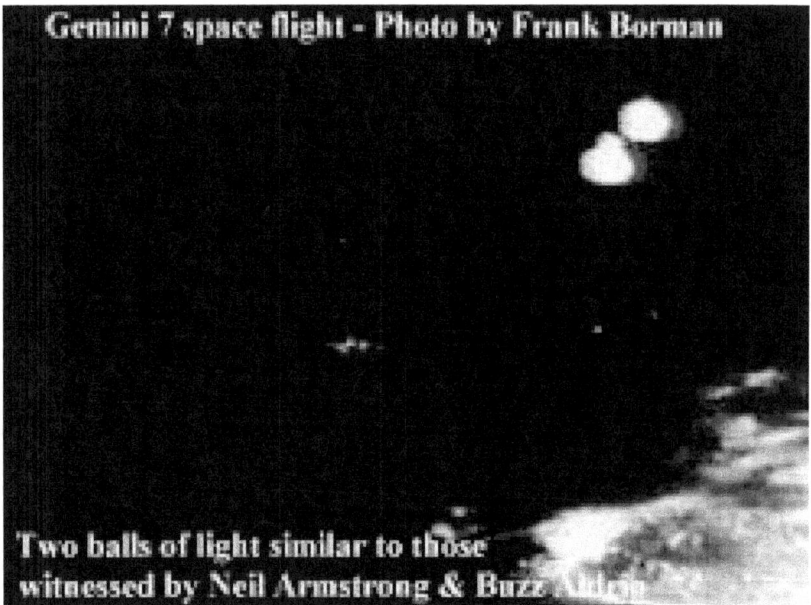

Gemini 7 space flight - Photo by Frank Borman

Two balls of light similar to those witnessed by Neil Armstrong & Buzz Aldrin

1965, SEPTEMBER 3 – In Exeter, New Hampshire an UFO
sighting by many locals and police is well publicized. The craft
was large and dark with flashing lights. The Air Force explains
it away as a "temperature inversion causing stars to twinkle."

The Exeter News-Letter.

ESTABLISHED 1831   Fourteen Pages   EXETER, N. H., THURSDAY, SEPT. 9, 1965   Ten Cents Per Copy   VOL. CXXXV ... NO. ?

Unidentified Flying Objects
Witnessed by Exeter Police

Exeter and Kensington were
centers of speculation over the
weekend following reports of
the sighting in two separate
places of brilliantly lighted

joined by Officer David Hunt.
Suddenly the UFO rose in a
blinding glow of red light from
behind a clump of trees.
Described as about the size

TOWN of Exeter

The Exeter News-Letter was
notified late last night that
the prime aircraft of the 100th

1965, NOVEMBER 8 – Dorothy Kilgallen, journalist and panelist on the TV show 'What's My Line' dies under mysterious circumstances from an apparent suicide at age 52. She was very outspoken about UFO secrecy in the 1950s and 1960s. She also knew and interviewed Marilyn Monroe and knew of government cover-ups, according to declassified DIA and FBI files. Dorothy was one of the last journalists to have interviewed Jack Ruby. The results of that interview never came out, but she stated months before her death that she was coming out with a story that "would blow the JFK case sky high, with information about UFOs as well."

1965, DECEMBER 6 – The Kecksburg UFO crash occurs with many town witnesses. It was a bell shaped craft with strange writing on it. The military sends in many personnel for the retrieval and quarantine the area. The official explanation was that it was a meteor. Local radio host, John Murphy, tries to do a radio documentary on the sighting, but is threatened by 'men in black.'

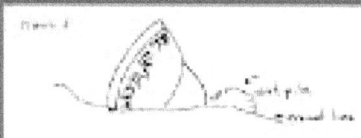

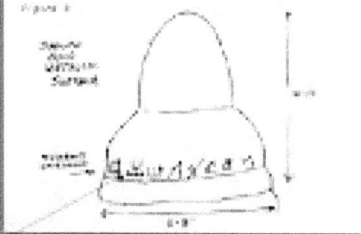

THEY DROVE IT OUT OF THE WOODS.
AND I'VE SEEN MANY ARMY TRUCKS.
THIS ONE HAD A WHITE STAR ON THE
SIDES. I REMEMBER VERY CLEARLY.

I WOULD SWEAR ON THE BIBLE AND
TAKE A LIE DETECTOR TEST.

YOURS TRULY
MR. JERRY BETTERS

5330 FERN ST. #405
PGH. PA. 15224

Attachment 13

1965 – U.S. Navy Operation 'Deepfreeze' in Antarctica sees an UFO. Brazilian scientist Dr. Rubens J. Villela and two others serving aboard the Admiralty Bay saw a silvery bullet UFO burst through 37 feet of ice and vanish in the sky. In an earlier March, 1961 Antarctic expedition he reported a sighting stating, "positively the colors, the configuration and contours of the object, as a bodied light, with geometric forms, did not seem to be from this world, and I did not know what could possibly reproduce it."

1966 – There was a spike in UFO sightings in Project Blue Book compared to the previous year and the year after.

1966, FEBRUARY 3 – Luna 9, a Russian spacecraft, made the first controlled rocket-assisted landing on the moon.

1966, MARCH 8 – The United States announces it will substantially increase the number of troops in Viet Nam.

1966, MARCH 16 – Gemini 8 is launched from the United States and is a manned mission to dock in space.

1966, MARCH – Dexter County, Michigan has UFO sightings of various shaped craft. This was well documented by over 100 locals and police. Gerald Ford, then a congressman, did not accept the Air Force's 'ridicule the witness' strategy. Dr. J Allen Hynek was brought in and used the 'swamp gas' explanation to debunk the sightings.

Hillsdale Residents Probe Area Skies In Search Of UFO Traffic

DESCRIBES UNIDENTIFIED FLYING OBJECT —"It was flat on the bottom and kind of high and peaked at the top," says Frank Manor, 47, of Dexter, as he described an unidentified flying object which he had sighted in a field on his farm near Ann Arbor. Manor's son, Ronald is at right.— (AP Wirephoto)

Reports Indicate 'Objects' Returned

The question of whether there are objects under control of intelligent beings from other planets coming to earth has been a source of conjecture and bewilderment to scientists and laymen for years.

But there are now people in the area who are no longer questioning if such objects exist. They are convinced. They say they have seen them.

Mrs. Jason Merrill, 263 Union St., her 12-year-old daughter, Susan and Mrs. Jimmie Jones, 276 Union St. are among the believers, and they support their belief with a detailed description of three objects they spotted northeast of Hillsdale between 7:30 and 8 Tuesday night.

The three give essentially the same description of three objects which hovered in a horizontal - triangular formation.

Mrs. Merrill said the objects stayed in formation for about 10 minutes. Then, two of the objects moved rapidly in a northeasterly direction, fading out of sight into the distance.

The other object remained, hovering with a flutterine mo-

Local Experts Discuss Sight

In an effort to find out what scientists think about unidentified flying objects (UFO) The Daily News talked with Dr. Chih-ha Wu Hsiung, head of the physics department of Hillsdale College and Prof. Tyler Pett, professor of physical science.

Dr. Hsiung said she has "no idea" what the objects are.

"I would not say this is impossible," she said, referring to the possibility of vehicles coming to earth from another planet.

Mr. Pett said that although he has been aware of UFO reports for 20 years he has never seen one.

Air Force Enters Mystery Of State's Flying Objects

ANN ARBOR (AP) — As reports of unidentified flying objects ... The Unidentified Flying Objects Office at Wright-Patterson AFB at Dayton, Ohio, asked ... ing he has heard indicates proof of "extraterrestial objects" any more than numerous other re ...

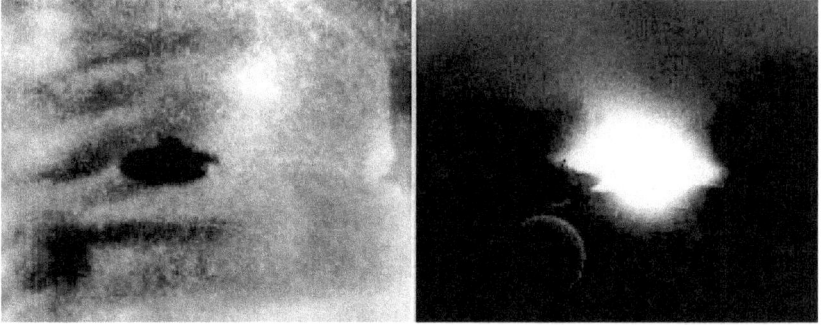

1966 Pictures of saucer landing on a road near Clare,
Michigan

1966, APRIL 5 – The Armed Services Committee conducts a formal hearing on UFOs. This was widely publicized with strong public and editorial criticism of the Air Force's handling of Project Blue Book. Gerald Ford, the house minority leader, supported this. Attendees included J. Allen Hynek, Major Hector Quintanilla, and Harold Brown. The result of the hearing was to do a scientific study by the Condon Committee at the University of Colorado. Donald Keyhoe claimed that this committee was run by the CIA.

1966, APRIL 10 – Luna 10 is launched from Russia and becomes the first man-made object to orbit the moon.

1966, JUNE 2 – Surveyor 1 is launched and becomes the first U.S. spacecraft to land on the moon.

1966, JULY 4 – North Viet Nam declares general mobilization.

1966, JULY 10 – Gemini 10 is launched and is another manned docking mission.

1966, AUGUST 10 – Lunar Orbiter 1 is launched. It is the first U.S. spacecraft to orbit the moon with the purpose of taking pictures and mapping the surface. Lunar Orbiter 2 was launched on November 6th later that year. The results were to be used to plan later manned Apollo missions to the moon.

1966, SEPTEMBER 12 - Gemini 11 is launched and is a manned docking mission.

1966, NOVEMBER 15 – Gemini 12 is launched and is a manned docking mission.

1966 – Alfred Kastler wins the Nobel Prize in Physics for combining magnetic resonance and optical resonance. This led to the development of lasers and masers (deep space spacecraft communication and radio telescopes).

1966 – The Condon Report (CIA run) declares "It is highly improbable UFOs exist" and debunk the phenomenon. At first they had everyone's support, but there was a mass exodus of objective scientists once they saw Condon's bias. This organization had the blessing from the congress and the military to finally look into the UFO phenomenon objectively.

1967 APRIL 27 – 'Look Magazine' publishes and article, 'The Flying Saucer Fiasco' exposing the bias of the Condon Committee, and was written by John Fuller. It cited firing of high-ranking staff and the near mutiny of the staff scientists.

CONDON REPORT REJECTED

UFO Group Here Hits Skeptics

1969, January 30th, 'The Pittsbugh Post-Gazette' article rejecting the Condon Report co-authored by Stanton Friedman

Doctor Edward Condon of the Condon Report

1967 – John Murphy announces he is reopening his investigation of the Kecksburg UFO case, but is struck by a car two days later and dies.

1967 – UFOs hover over Malmstrom Nuclear Ballistic Missile Base in Great Falls, Montana. According to witnesses, up to 20 missiles were shut down one by one. Boeing, the manufacturers of the silos, could not explain how they were shut down after their investigation. The Air force then created a cover story. A similar silo shutdown occurred in 1966 at Minot AFB in North Dakota with witnesses and NORAD radar evidence. There were reports of this happening in Russia as well.

1967 – The Society for the Investigating of the Unexplained (SITU) is formed in New Jersey by Ivan T. Sanderson and his wife, Alma. This is a citizen's group. Sanderson was educated at Eton with two masters degrees from Cambridge University, Great Britain. By this time he had become a senior authority on the unexplained with extensive UFO research. He did thorough research of the Flatwoods Monster sightings of 1952.

1967, JUNE 23 – Frank Edwards, radio host and UFO researcher dies of a heart attack at age 58. Earlier in March he met with Donald Keyhoe and said that he was working on an upcoming expose of the Condon Committee that was highly critical. Edwards also said to Keyhoe that NICAP should not be involved with the Condon people because they were not to be trusted. Edwards had been doing lectures and fought against UFO censorship by the 'military-industrial complex.' Edwards was also the famous radio host who broke the news story about Eisenhower's meeting with extraterrestrials in 1954 at Muroc AFB.

President Truman and radio host Frank Edwards

1967, SEPTEMBER 9 – The first case of animal mutilation in Southern Colorado is publicized.

1967, AUGUST – NICAP withdraws support of the Condon Committee.

1968, JULY 29 – There is a formal open hearing and six scientists testify about UFOs before the U.S. House of Representatives Committee in Science and Astronautics. Among the scientist attendees were Dr. J. Allen Hynek of Project Blue Book, Dr. Carl Sagan, Dr. James McDonald, Dr. Robert Hall, Dr. James Harder, and Dr. Robert Baker. Among the scientists who submitted written statements were Dr. Donald Menzel, Stanton Friedman, Dr. Roger Shepard, Dr. R. Leo Sprinkle, Dr. Gary Henderson, and Dr. Frank Salisbury. The hearing was intended to debunk UFO sightings and reduce civilian interest in the subject, despite the presentations of serious researchers. As could be predicted, MJ-12 member Dr. Donald Menzel thought any consideration of the problem was a complete waste of time.

1968 – Major General Richard O'Keefe, Air Force special investigator and Acting Inspector General, creates a standing order for all Air Force base commanders, "what is required is that every UFO sighting be investigated and reported to the Air Technical Intelligence Center (ATIC) at Wright-Patterson AFB."

1968 - UFOs are spotted in Viet Nam during the Tet Offensive. When UFOs were fired upon the UFOs returned fire with the same military rounds and missiles to the military troops. U.S. command then orders the military not to shoot at the UFOs. General George S. Brown admits at a press conference that UFOs caused much interference and that a battle with them occurred in 1968.

1969, JANUARY 20 – Richard Nixon takes office as President of The United States until August 9, 1974. He knows much about the UFO phenomenon because of his early days as Vice

110

President to President Eisenhower. President Lyndon B. Johnson steps down after one term and does not seek reelection.

1969, ALL YEAR – The U.S. government under President Nixon takes the position to suppress all UFO information instead of investigating it, according to UFO historian Richard Dolan.

1969, JANUARY 11 – The Condon Report releases their report findings that UFOs do not exist and states that further studies on the subject are no longer needed.

1969, FEBRUARY – 'Star Trek,' the original series, is cancelled by NBC after 79 episodes, despite its growing popularity, a significant letter-writing campaign by fans, and protests by creator Gene Roddenberry. The network blamed the cancellation on poor ratings. What was not mentioned at the time was that NBC kept moving the show to poorer time slots and that the rating system used was not comprehensive enough by today's standards.

1969 – The Science Applications International Corporation (SAIC) is formed in Mclean, Virginia by Robert Beyster. It provides government services, information technology, and engineering to the U.S. intelligence community, including the NSA.

1969, MAY 31 – The Mutual UFO Network (MUFON) is formed by Walt Andrus and Allen Utke, along with many members from APRO. This is a citizen's group.

1969, July 16 – The U.S. Congress passes a federal law in The Code of Federal Regulations, document title 14, section 1211.108. This makes it illegal for an American to contact an extraterrestrial with punishment of a $5000 fine and a one year jail sentence.

1969, JULY 21 – Apollo 11 was the first manned flight to land on the moon. Many astronauts in the space program had UFO sightings in space up to this point and NASA was involved in the cover-up. NASA also states today that they have lost all audio tapes of this first landing. Hundreds of HAM operators on earth claim to have heard the astronauts discussing the presence of UFOs on the moon on a secured channel. Some astronauts, such as Edgar Mitchell and Gordon Cooper, were very outspoken about the presence of extraterrestrials here on earth. The computer capabilities on Apollo 11 were very antiquated by today's standards with only 72 Kbytes of memory.

1969 Apollo 11 pictures transmitted to Swiss TV uncensored

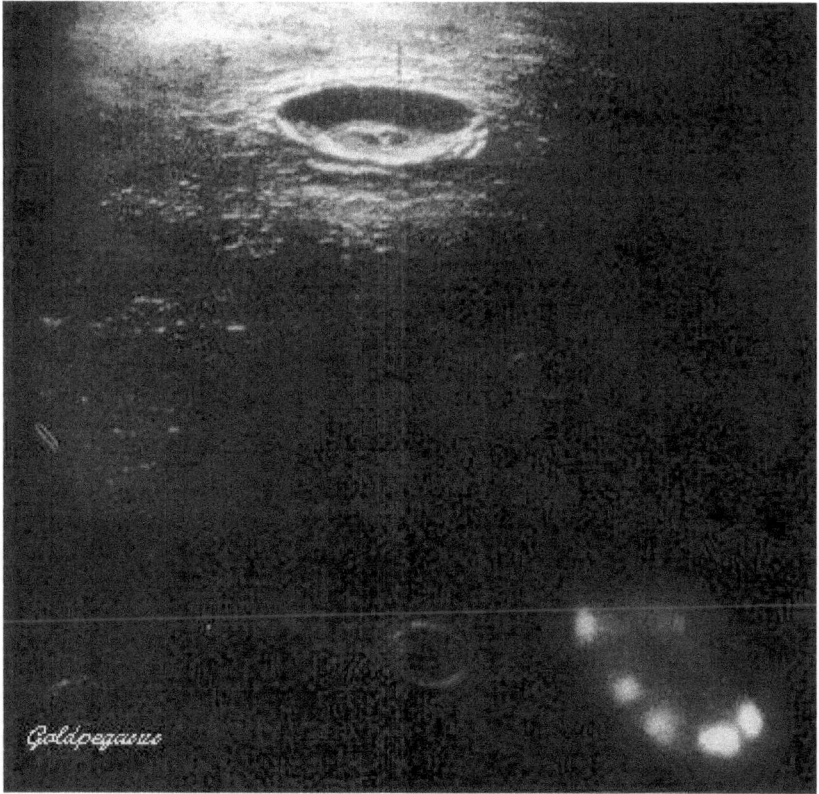

1971 Apollo 14 NASA moon landing photo

113

Apollo 14 moon picture with Edgar Mitchell's signature

1969, OCTOBER 20 - The Bollender Memo is written to explain the proper reporting channels for UFO sightings in the military. It also explains that UFO reports are a matter of national security and no longer part of the Blue Book system. This was part of the Joint Army-Navy-Air Force publication 146(e), Canadian-United States Communications Instructions for Reporting Vital Intelligence Sightings (CIRVIS). This reporting system is still in effect today under NORAD and this joint Canadian/United States organization is exempt from the Freedom of Information Act. Air Force General Carroll Bollender was also an engineer for the lunar excursion module for the first moon landing in 1969.

1969, DECEMBER 27 – James E. McDonald presents a paper to the American Association for the Advancement of Science titled 'Science in Default: Twenty-two Years of Inadequate UFO Investigations.' This was a thoroughgoing criticism of the Condon Committee and Project Blue Book.

1970, JANUARY 20 – Project Blue Book was closed citing the Condon Report. Their final position was that UFOs do not exist.

1970 – The FAA in section 9-8-1 of their 'Rules and Regulations' states that all pilots are not to report UFO sightings.

1970 – Many classified nuclear space aircraft systems programs have been cancelled by large aerospace companies by the this time according to researcher Stanton Friedman, a nuclear physicist.

1970 – Intel develops the first dynamic access memory chip (DRAM). IBM introduces semiconductor memory, replacing magnetic core memory.

1970 – Ivan T. Sanderson and his wife Alma are diagnosed with brain cancer simultaneously. Sanderson claims that he and his wife had been targeted. They both die within two and a half years. This occurred at the height of his career when SITU was having significant increases in membership and when he was making weekly high profile appearances on major radio and TV shows, such as the Dick Cavett Show. SITU closed down after their deaths. The CIA had a presence at his New Jersey facility with resident staff member Richard T. Grybos. Sanderson's 1967 book, 'Uninvited Visitors: a Biologist Looks at UFOs' was well received and examined many cases, as well as a discussion of the Philadelphia Experiment.

1971, APRIL – 'Industrial Research,' an engineering research magazine polled its members and 80% rejected the Condon Report findings, 76% believed that the government was concealing the UFO facts, and 32% believed that UFOs were extraterrestrial.

1971, JUNE 13 – James E. McDonald commits suicide after first being declared mentally unstable. He was one of the leading scientists of APRO and one of the six scientists testifying before congress in 1968. After visiting Write-Patterson AFB and studying Project Blue Book he declared that Project Blue Book was not including the most significant cases and that the Air Force was debunking the reports. McDonald released to the public 'The Trick Memo,' which outlined the Condon Report's strategy of debunking the UFO phenomenon. This memo was written by Dr. Robert Low, one of the investigators for Condon who had become disenchanted with Condon. Edward Condon tried, unsuccessfully, to get McDonald fired from his tenured faculty position at the University of Arizona. McDonald held a Ph.D. in physics and was an expert in supersonic transport.

MUTUAL UFO NETWORK
UFO JOURNAL

Dr. James E. McDonald

Audio Recordings by:
Dr. James McDonald
Senior Physicist, Institute of Atmospheric Physics
University of Arizona - Tuscon

Tape 7   Side 1 & 2
7 inch Reel   Speed: 3 3/4 ips
Time: 66:12

Disc 9

Incident at Vandenberg Air Force Base Part 1
Lompoc, California
Friday, October 6, 1967
Supplied by: John L. Pare

Ivan T. Sanderson in his home office, *circa* **1965.**

1971, SEPTEMBER 30 - President Nixon and Russia's Leonid Brezhnev sign an agreement designed to minimize the potential for nuclear war as it relates to anti-ballistic missile systems. This was part of the SALT I negotiations. In article three it states, "The parties undertake to notify each other in the event of detections by warning systems of unidentified objects …"

1971 – IBM invents the floppy disc.

1972, JANUARY 1 – The Defense Mapping Agency is created with its headquarters at the U.S. Naval Observatory in Washington D.C. Its purpose is to generate information from satellites using advanced imagery.

1972 – Stanford Research Institute Remote Viewing Program is established in Menlo Park, California by the CIA. The purpose was for psychic spying on enemies and remote viewing extraterrestrials, according to Ingo Swann and other psychic participants. Ingo Swann reported seeing structures and other life entities on the far side of the moon as well as extraterrestrial bases on earth. All of the psychics there remote viewed extraterrestrials at some point. Swann's 1998 book, 'Penetration: The Question of Extraterrestrial and Human Telepathy,' details some of these experiences.

1972, DECEMBER 7 - Apollo 17 was the last manned flight to the moon. Although 20 flights were scheduled with space craft already built, remaining missions were cancelled. Some researchers speculate that it was because we were "warned off the moon" by alien spacecraft observed during the Apollo 11 original landing.

1972 – Doctor J. Allen Hynek states , "NICAP and APRO are the two best UFO groups of their time, consisting of serious sober minded people capable of valuable contributions to the subject." Dr. Hynek was the main scientific consultant of Project Sign, Project Grudge, and Project Blue Book. In his later years Hynek became sympathetic to public disclosure.

1972 – Dr. Gordon J. F. McDonald testifies before the House Subcommittee on Oceans and International Environment that there are electromagnetic weapons used for mind control and mental disruption.

1973, FEBRUARY 19 – President Nixon with close friend/actor Jackie Gleason secretly go to Homestead Air force Base in Florida. Gleason saw the bodies of small aliens in glass topped refrigerators. He was emotionally shaken by the experience. This was reported by his wife of the time, Beverly McKittrick, to an interviewer with 'Esquire Magazine.' She also mentions this in her unpublished manuscript called, 'The Great One.' Gleason also shared the details of this event with Larry Warren, member of Air Force Security at RAF Bentwaters in 1986.

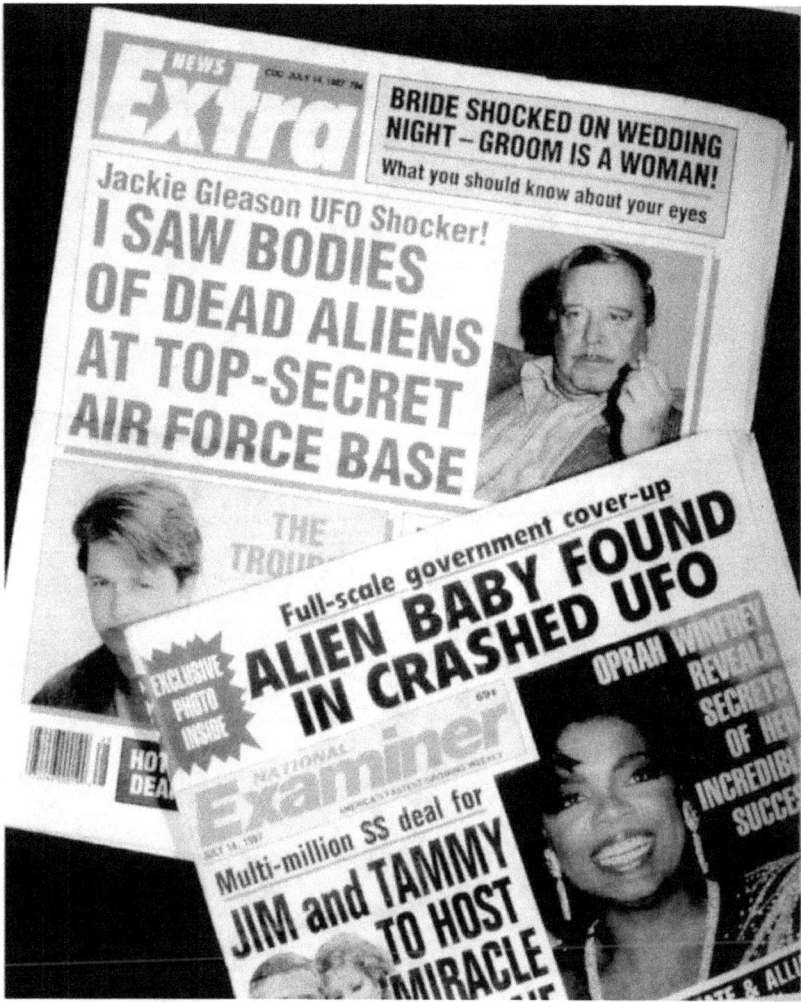

Tabloid examples of how the media diffuses a serious UFO
claim and attacks one's credibility

AUG.13.2002   4:08PM   NO.555   P.2

ENQUIRER EXCLUSIVE: His Ex-Wife Reveals . . .

Jackie Gleason actually saw space aliens and believes he lived before as a swashbuckling English duke, reveals his ex-wife Beverly, who was married to the comic from 1970 through 1974. Those are just two of the sensational revelations from a book she's writing that shows "The Great One" — or Jack as

she calls him — as he's never been seen before. Gleason declined repeated attempts by The ENQUIRER to interview him about the book. Here, in a sneak preview of her blockbuster book, Beverly tells about Gleason's incredible encounter with aliens ... exclusively for ENQUIRER readers.

ENQ. 8/16/83

Jackie Gleason Saw Bodies of Space Aliens at Air Force Base

By BEVERLY GLEASON

Space aliens exist! Ask Jackie Gleason — he's actually seen them.

I'll never forget the night in 1973 my famous husband came home, slumped white-faced in an armchair and spilled out the incredible story to me.

He was late. It was around 11:30 p.m. and I'd been worried. As soon as I heard his key turn in the lock of our golf course home in Inverrary, Fla., I jumped to my feet and asked, "Where have you been?"

His reply stunned me:

"I've been at Homestead Air Force Base — and I've seen the bodies of some aliens from outer space.

President Nixon Arranged for Him To See Them

"It's top secret. Only a few people know. But the President arranged for me to be escorted in there and see them."

I knew that he and President Nixon were buddies, so that didn't surprise me. But the story that followed was incredible.

"No one would tell me the full details, but a spacecraft has obviously crashed near here," said Jack.

"When I arrived at the base, I was given a heavily armed military escort and driven to a building in a remote area.

"We had to pass a guard at the door, then were shown into a large room.

"And there were the aliens, lying on four separate tables.

"They were tiny — only about two feet tall — with small bald heads and disproportionately large ears.

"They must have been dead for some time because they'd been embalmed."

I started to smile. It seemed just too much to believe.

But Jack caught my look and stared at me for a long time, his face haggard.

"It sounds incredible, but I swear it's true," he said. "I'll never forget it ... ever."

It was something that had a profound effect on him. He had obviously been sworn to secrecy, and perhaps regretted even telling me, his wife, because he would never dis-

belief in the occult and in UFOs.

He read anything he could get his hands on about new UFO sightings around the world.

"You see — there's another one," he'd say, pointing to an article about a sighting.

He was fiercely patriotic and even paid his taxes happily.

But one thing he detested about the government was what he called its cover-up on UFOs.

"They know all about them," he'd say angrily. "So why do they keep denying that they exist and painting people who believe in them as idiots?"

He believed that the gov-

coming from a friendly place, and we should communicate with them," he'd insist.

And he was triumphant when his own beliefs were bolstered by a backstage meeting with one of the astronauts.

Jack was co-hosting a TV show, and one of the guests this night was one of the early American adventurers in space.

When the show was over, Jack and the astronaut became absorbed in a private discussion about UFOs. And when Jack told the man that he was a believer in UFOs, the astronaut confided to him:

"You're right. They do

A FIRM BELIEVER in UFOs, Jackie Gleason actually saw the bodies of space aliens, according to his ex-wife Beverly, shown at left with Gleason as they posed happily on their wedding day.

exist. I've seen one with my own eyes during our mission.

"But we've been sworn to secrecy, and the government will never let the information out to the public."

Jack was thrilled — and furious. He was thrilled to be proved right at last, furious to have his theories about a cover-up confirmed.

And, of course, actually seeing the bodies of those aliens was the final proof.

He's intrigued by anything involving the psychic and the occult. He has thousands of books in his library and many of them deal with supernatural subjects.

There was no doubt in Jack's mind that he had lived before, as a swashbuckling English duke in the days of King Henry VIII.

His life as a 16th-century duke had evidently been just as exciting as his present one. He'd tell me how, in his nighttime dreams he rode into battle, dressed in a suit of gleaming armor and mounted on a snow white horse. Of course, he was always victorious.

And through his dreams he would recall how he lived in a huge castle and about all the servants he had and people who owed their allegiance to him.

"I've lived before," Jack told me. "I haven't the

Some researchers claim that the CIA heavily influences 'The National Enquirer' articles

1973 – MUFON investigates the Aurora, Texas UFO crash of 1897. This was a report of an UFO crash and a town burial of a small alien being. There were local 1897 newspaper articles discussing the event. During the investigation the gravestone with an engraving of the alien aircraft disappeared and the grave was exhumed by an unknown party.

Photo of Aurora, Texas UFO crash headstone of alien pilot, now missing

A Windmill Demolishes It.

Aurora, Wise Co., Tex., April 17.—(To The News.)—About 6 o'clock this morning the early risers of Aurora were astonished at the sudden appearance of the airship which has been sailing through the country.

It was traveling due north, and much nearer the earth than ever before. Evidently some of the machinery was out of order, for it was making a speed of only ten or twelve miles an hour and gradually settling toward the earth. It sailed directly over the public square, and when it reached the north part of town collided with the tower of Judge Proctor's windmill and went to pieces with a terrific explosion, scattering debris over several acres of ground, wrecking the windmill and water tank and destroying the judge's flower garden.

The pilot of the ship is supposed to have been the only one on board, and while his remains are badly disfigured, enough of the original has been picked up to show that he was not an inhabitant of this world.

Mr. T. J. Weems, the United States signal service officer at this place and an authority on astronomy, gives it as his opinion that he was a native of the planet Mars.

Papers found on his person—evidently the record of his travels—are written in some unknown hieroglyphics, and can not be deciphered.

The ship was too badly wrecked to form any conclusion as to its construction or motive power. It was built of an unknown metal, resembling somewhat a mixture of aluminum and silver, and it must have weighed several tons.

The town is full of people to-day who are viewing the wreck and gathering specimens of the strange metal from the debris. The pilot's funeral will take place at noon to-morrow.   S. E. HAYDON.

1897 Aurora Newspaper article

124

1973 – Colonel Joseph Bryan III, former head of the CIA Psychological Warfare Division, manages to discredit Donald Keyhoe, take over NICAP, debunk it, and eventually close it down. John L Acuff became director. He and all following directors had CIA ties.

1973 – J. Allen Hynek forms CUFOS, Center for UFO Studies, in Evanston, Illinois.

1973 – The Trilateral Commision is formed by David Rockefeller as a non-partison discussion group to foster closer cooperation with North America, Western Europe, and Japan. They are the liberal, globalist, internationalist, intellectual elite, and many are members of the Bilderberg Group, as well as the Council on Foreign Relations.

1973 – Xerox develops the Ethernet for connecting multiple computers.

1974, August 9 – President Richard Nixon leaves office.

1974, October 17 – Major UFO sightings occurred within a 24 hour period. Over 50 U.S. cities and towns reported concentrated UFO activity with craft being seen of all shapes and sizes. Hundreds of reports went to MUFON and other UFO organizations. John Chancellor of NBC News covered the sightings for several nights on television. The U.S. Air Force stated that the subject of UFOs was unworthy of further scientific research since the closing of Project Blue Book in 1969. That same year Senator Barry Goldwater wanted some answers to these sightings and the UFO phenomenon, but was denied access to Wright-Patterson AFB and to any UFO information. His personal friend, retired Air Force General Curtis Lemay, one of the military keepers of the secrecy, scolded Goldwater for having tried to acquire any information on the subject. In Leonard Stringfield's 1977 book, 'Situation Red, the UFO Siege!' he gives specifics of this event, as well as other well documented cases. Goldwater testified to his encounter with Lemay on various video interviews.

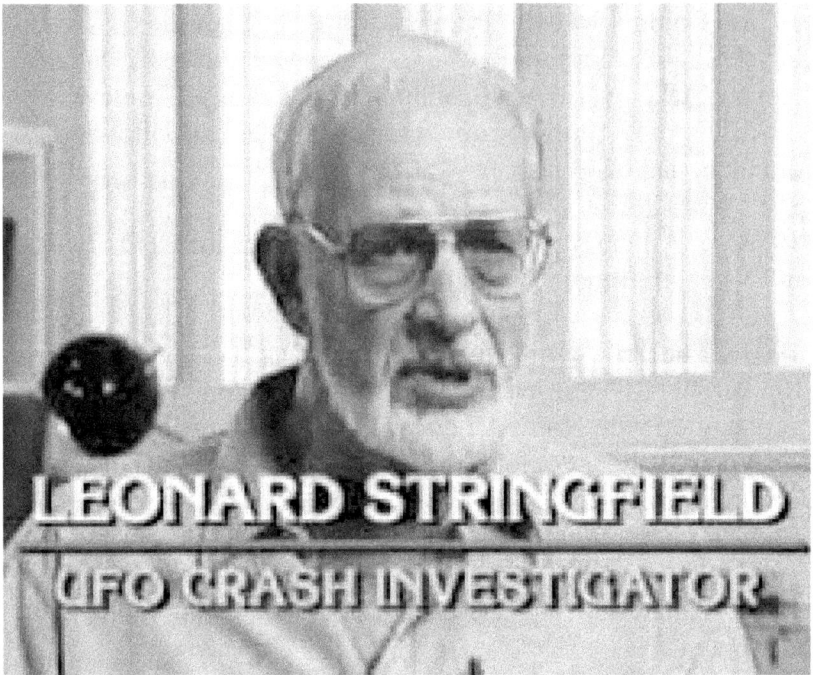

LEONARD STRINGFIELD
UFO CRASH INVESTIGATOR

1974 – The first personal computers are introduced to the market.

CONCLUSION

Astronaut Edgar D. Mitchell wrote in his 2008 book, 'The Way of The Explorer: An Apollo Astronaut's Journey Through the Material and Mystical World,' the followings:

> "Yes, there have been ET visitations. There have been crashed craft. There have been material and bodies recovered. There has been a certain amount of reverse engineering that has allowed some of these craft, or some components, to be duplicated. And there is some group of people that may or may not be associated with the government at this point that have this knowledge. They have been attempting to conceal this knowledge. People in high level government have very little, if any, valid information about this. It has been the subject of disinformation in order to deflect attention and create confusion so the truth doesn't come out."

CIA, military intelligence, secret security from some of the large multinational companies, the Bilderberg Group, the Trilateral Commission, The Council on Foreign Relations, and certain international organizations in the Western world (oil and banking cartels) control the secrecy according to former Canadian Associate Minister of National Defense, Paul Hellyer. Hellyer calls this the "shadow government" in his 2010 book, 'Light at The End of The Tunnel.' Major Donald E. Keyhoe declared that the CIA is the power behind the secrecy. Cold war Historian Richard Dolan stated that the global, multinational banks are at the core of the power elite.

There are many examples of how certain intelligence agencies operate. Researchers have stated and I have observed that they infiltrate UFO citizen group meetings, create chaos, create confusion, create distractions, introduce misinformation, and try to discredit authentic UFO researchers. One example is introducing obvious faked UFO pictures with authentic UFO pictures so that all of the pictures are dismissed. One distraction is stating that our black budget technology is so advanced and wound in secrecy that no one will ever understand it. There are stories advanced that the Nazis had operational flying saucers before the end of the war, worked with extraterrestrials, and were based in Antarctica in the mid 1940s. In 2015 the CIA announced that all of the UFO sightings of the 1950s and 1960s were of U.S. experimental craft. This was presented on the major television news networks. One of the major deceptions presented is that The United States had secret advanced technology far beyond what was presented to the public and scientific establishment. This supposed secret advanced technology is used to explain sightings in the 1940s, 1950s, and 1960s, even suggesting that we had bases on the moon at that time. This would explain the anomalous structures found on the moon. If one looks at the actual pace of scientific development and manufacturing capabilities during those times one sees that this is a farfetched notion. More importantly, one must consider UFO sightings before 1900. The official explanations of UFO sightings rarely come close to the actual witness testimonies. There is an ongoing debunking of significant sightings, such as the Phoenix Lights of 1997. These were two one-mile long, silent, boomerang shaped craft moving very slowly without sound, and seen by 10,000 people, including the governor. In the past they explained this as swamp gas, Venus, balloons, or birds. Ridicule of the subject and witnesses is the norm. One crazy story is that aliens are digesting our souls through ancient structures on the moon. Others state there are secret rogue treaties with bad aliens allowing for human experimentation.

The power elite also control the media, such as NASA not allowing live television feeds from space. Of course they want to create an image of the extraterrestrials as evil and as a threat, so if needed they can weaponize against them. Now we have pseudo researchers who say that we should throw out all early UFO research and start from scratch. Every year in the United States there are about 6000 reported sightings of UFOs to the authorities and to organizations such as MUFON and the National UFO Reporting Center. There has been a slow, secretive, and methodical effort to eliminate or distort unwanted written, video, audio, and digital media through the years. Why are the NASA audio tapes of Apollo 11, the first moon landing, missing? Why is psychic Ingo Swan's book about telepathic communication with extraterrestrials out of print? Why are

128

some convincing UFO pictures I saw on the internet years ago no longer there? I could go on.

In 2011 the Obama administration reported their official statement through the White House Office of Science and Technology Policy:

> "The U.S. Government has no evidence that any life exists outside our planet, or that an extraterrestrial presence has contacted or engaged any member of the human race. In addition, there is no credible information to suggest that any evidence is being hidden from the public eye."

In a 1993 alumni speech for UCLA Ben Rich, CEO and president of Lockheed Skunk Works, said, "We now have the technology to take ET home." Lord Desmond Leslie, relative of Winston Churchill and ufologist did a film in 1990 called, 'UFOs, The Contacts,' by Michael Hesemann. He stated that the reason for the UFO secrecy was because of "free energy, the end of the oil monopoly, aviation as we know it, and the automotive industry."

There are currently seventeen separate intelligence agencies in the United States. Many believe at this point in our U.S. history that the UFO secrecy has everything to do with money, control, and power, despite the ruling elite's desire to have us believe that knowledge of extraterrestrials would be too traumatic for the people of the world to endure. This was the opinion of former CIA Intelligence Officer Victor Marchetti. He joined the agency in 1955 and became Special Assistant to the Deputy Director of the CIA, Richard M. Holms, from 1966 to 1969. Marchetti became disenchanted with the CIA and resigned in 1969. He expressed his sentiment in a May, 1979 article published in 'Second Look' magazine titled, 'How the CIA Views the UFO Phenomenon.' The following are excerpts from the article he wrote:

> "I do know that the CIA and U.S. Government have been concerned over the UFO phenomenon for many years and that their attempts, both past and recent, to discount the significance of the phenomenon and to explain away the apparent lack of official interest in it have all the ear-markings of a classic intelligence cover-up. The purpose

of the international conspiracy is to maintain workable stability among the nations of the world and for them, in turn, to retain institutional control over their respective populations. If the existence of UFOs were to be officially confirmed, a chain reaction could be initiated that would result in the collapse of the Earth's present power structure."

After completing this book I am now less confused. It took me on a journey to a place I had not anticipated, a look into the serious conspiratorial nature of UFO secrecy in The United States. It has everything to do with what is going on in the world today.

BIBLIOGRAPHY

Authors note: This is a listing of the books and some of the sources used for this study. I do not necessarily agree with all of the ideas or facts presented in them. Some of these books helped shape the direction of my book by giving me a broader perspective of the subject.

Anonymous. 2015. *Anonymous CIA Agent Reveals the Truth about UFOs.* Micro Publishing Media, Inc.

Arnold, Kenneth. 1952. *The Coming of The Saucers.* Legend Press.

Air Force Regulation AFR 200-2. 1954. Military document dated August 12.

Bender, Albert. 1962. *Flying Saucers and the Three Men.* Saucerian Books.

Braun, Wernher von. 1952. *Man Will Conquer Space Soon.* Colliers Magazine.

Byrne & Hoffman. 1996. *Governing the Atom: The Politics of Risk.* Transaction Publishers.

Cameron, Grant. The Presidents UFO Website.

Chatelain, Albert. 1975. *Our Ancestors Came From Outer Space.* Doubleday and Company.

Chop. Albert. 1956. *'UFOs, The True Story of Flying Saucers.'* A major semi-documentary film by United Artists.

Clark, Jerome. 1990. *The UFO Encyclopedia: The Phenomenon From the Beginning.* Omnigraphics.

Code of Federal Regulations. 1969. Government document title 14, Section 1211.108. About military UFO reporting protocol.

Cook, Nick. 2001. *The Hunt for Zero Point.* Broadway Books.

Cooper, Gordon. 2000. *Leap of Faith: An Astronaut's Journey Into the Unknown.* Harper.

Cremo, Michael and Thompson, Richard L. 1993. *Forbidden Archeology.* Torchlight Publishing.

Daily Mirror. 1980. *'Secret Meetings to Shape the World.'* Newspaper article on February 13.

Daily Star. 1952. *'CAA Radar Man Tracks Flying Saucers Over Washington, Can't Explain Them.'* Sudbury, Ontario newspaper article on July 31.

Dolan, Richard. 2000. *UFOs and the National Security State.* Keyhole Publishing.

Dolan, Richard. 2014. *UFOS for the 21st Century Mind: A Fresh guide to an Ancient Mystery.* CreateSpace Independent Publishing Platform.

Desmond, Leslie. 1953. *Flying Saucers Have Landed.* British Book Center.

Desmond, Leslie. 1990. *UFO Contacts.* Film by Michael Hesemann shown on American and British television.

Edwards, Frank. 1964. *Strange World.* Citadel Press.

Edwards, Frank. 1966. *Flying Saucers, Serious Business.* Citadel Press.

El Mercurio. 1947. *'El Admirante Richard E. Byrd sa Retiere a la Importancia Estralegica de los Pelos.'* Chilean newspaper article in March.

Encyclopedia Britannica

Estulin, Daniel. 2005. *The True Story of the Bilderberg Group.* Timeday LLC.

FAA Rules and Regulations. 1970. Section 9-8-1. Prohibits pilots from reporting UFO sightings.

Fall River Newspaper. 1952. *'Jets Told to Shoot Down Flying Saucers – Air Force Puzzled but no Longer Skeptical.'* Newspaper article on July 28.

Fort, Charles. 1919. *The Book of the Damned.* Cosimo Classics.

Freshino, Frank C. 2007. *Shoot Them Down! The Flying Saucer Air Wars of 1952.* LuLu Enterprises.

Friedman, Stanton. 1992. *'Recollections of Roswell.'* Video for Home Box Office on American television.

Friedman, Stanton. 1997. *Crash at Carona.* Marlowe and Company.

Friedman, Stanton. 2005. *Top Secret/Majic.* Da Capo Press.

Friedman, Stanton. 2007. *Captured! The Betty and Barney Hill UFO Experience: The True Story of the World's First Documented Alien Abduction.* New Page Books.

Friedman, Stanton. 2008. *Flying Saucers and Science.* New Page Books.

Fuller, John G. 1966. *The Interrupted Journey: Two lost Hours Aboard a Flying Saucer.* Dial Press.

Greenwald, John. 2002. *Beyond the UFO Secrecy.* The Black Vault.

Greer, Steven M. 2001. *Disclosure.* Carden Jennings Publishing.

Haines, Richard F. 1999. *CE-5 Close Encounters of the Fifth Kind.* Source Books.

Hillenkoetter, Roscoe. 1960. '*Air Force Order on 'Saucers Cited.'* New York Times Newspaper article on February 27.

Hillsdale Daily News. 1966. *'Hillsdale Residents Probe Area Skies in Search of UFO Traffic.'* Frontpage newspaper article on March 23.

Hellyer, Paul. 2010. *Light at the End of the Tunnel.* Author House.

Imbrogno, Philip. 2008. *Interdimensional Universe.* L. Lewellyn Publications.

Herald Express. 1947. *'Flying Saucers Found.'* Frontpage newspaper article on July 8.

Jacobs, David. 1975. *The UFO Controversy in America.* Temple University.

Jessup, M. K. 1955. *The Case for the UFO.* New Saucerian Books.

JANAP. 1954. JANAP 146C. Joint Army-Navy-Air Force Publication on March 10.

JANAP. 1969. 'Bollender memo JANAP 146E. Joint Army-Navy-Air Force Publication.

Kendrick, Frazier. 1991. *The Hundredth Monkey: and other Paradigms of the Paranormal.* Prometheus Books.

Keyhoe, Donald E. 1950. *The Flying Saucers are Real.* Fawcett Publications.

Keyhoe, Donald E. 1953. *Flying Saucers from Outer Space.* Henry Holt and Company.

Keyhoe, Donald E. 1955. *The Flying Saucer Conspiracy.* Henry Holt and Company.

Keyhoe, Donald E. 1960. *Flying Saucers: Top secret.* New York: Putnam.

Keyhoe, Donald E. 1973. *Aliens from Space ...The Real Story of Unidentified Flying Objects.* Doubleday and Company.

Lorenzen, Jim and Coral. 1967. *Flying Saucer Occupants.* The New American Library.

Life Magazine. 1952. '*There is a Case for Interplanetary Saucers.*' Magazine article on April 7.

Los Angeles Examiner. 1942. '*Air Battle Rages Over Los Angeles.*' Frontpage newspaper article on February 26.

Los Angeles Times. 1942. '*L A. Area Raided!*' Frontpage newspaper article on February 26.

Los Angeles Times. 1942. '*Army Says Alarm Real.*' Frontpage newspaper article in February.

Las Vegas Sun. 1962. '*Brilliant Explosion Flares in Las Vegas Sky.*' Frontpage newspaper article in April.

Maccabee, Bruce. 2014. *The FBI CIA UFO Connection.* Richard Dolan Press.

Marchetti, Victor 1979. '*How the CIA Views the UFO Phenomenon.*' Second Look Magazine article in May.

McDonald, James E. 1969. '*Science in Default: Twenty-two Years of UFO investigations.*' Paper presented to the American Association for the Advancement of Science on December 27.

McMoneagle, Joseph. 2006. *Memoirs of a Psychic Spy.* Hampton Road Publishing.

Mitchell, Edgar D. 2008. *The Way of the Explorer: An Apollo Astronauts Journey Through the Material and Mystical Worlds.* New Page Books.

MUFON website. MUFON.com. Mutual UFO Network.

National Military Establishment Office of Public Information. 1949. 'Project Grudge.' United States Military.

NATO report. 1964. 'An Assessment.' Government document.

NICAP website. NICAP.org.

New York Herald Tribune. 1955. '*Conquest of Gravity Top Aim of Top Scientists in U.S.*' Newspaper article on November 20.

New York Times. 1944 '*Floating Mystery Ball is New Nazi Air Weapon.*' Frontpage newspaper article on December 14.

New York Times, 1945. '*Balls of Fire Stalk U.S. Fighters in Night Assault Over Germany.*' Newspaper article on January 2.

New York Times. 1952. '*Strange Objects in U.S Sky Observed by Radar.*' Frontpage newspaper articles on July 20 and 22.

Pittsburgh Post-Gazette. 1969. '*UFO Group Here Hits Skeptics.*' Newspaper article on January 30.

Project Sign. 1948. *'Estimate of the Situation.'* Government document.

Purdue University Website.

Randles, Jenny. 1995. *UFO: Crash Retrievals.* Blandford Press.

Randle, Kevin D. 1995. *A History of UFO Crashes.* Avon Publishers.

Randle, Kevin D. 2001. *Invasion Washington, UFOS Over the Capitol.* Harper Collins.

Randle, Kevin D. 2010. *Crash.* The Career Press.

Roswell Daily Record. 1947. *'RAAF Captures Flying Saucer on Ranch in Roswell Region.'* Frontpage newspaper article on July 8.

Ruppelt, Edward. 1955. *The Report on Unidentified Flying Objects.* Doubleday and Company.

Rutledge, Harley D. 1982. *Project Identification: The First Scientific Field Study of UFO Phenomena.* Prentice Hall Trade.

Sanderson, Ivan T. 1967. *Uninvited Visitors.* Crowles Education Corporation.

Sanderson, Ivan T. 1970. *Invisible Residents.* Adventures Unlimited Press.

San Francisco Call. 1896. *'A Winged Ship in the Sky.'* Frontpage article of newspaper on November 23.

San Francisco Examiner. 1952. *'The Air Force Today Revealed That Jet Pilots Have Been Placed on Twenty Four Hour Alert Against Flying Saucers.'* Newspaper article on July 29.

Seattle Post-Intelligencer. 1952. *'Air Force Orders Jet Pilots to Shoot Down Flying Saucers if They Refuse to Land.'* Newspaper article on July 29.

Smith, Paul Blake. 2016. *M041 The Bombshell Before Roswell.* W & B Publishers, Inc.

Smith, Wilbert. 1996. *The Boys From Topside.* Inner Light.

Star Trek Conventions. Speaking with actors and creators.

Steiger, Brad. 1976. *Project Blue Book.* Ballantine Books.

Stringfield, Leonard H. 2015. *UFO Crash Retrievals I through VII (series).* Saucerian Press.

Stringfield, Leonard H. 1977. *Situation Red, The UFO Siege!* Doubleday and Company.

Stone, Clifford. 2011. *Eyes Only.* Clifford Earl Stone.

Swann, Ingo. 1988. *Penetration: The Question of Extraterrestrial and Human Telepathy.* Ingo Swann Books.

Time Magazine. 1952. *'There is a Case for Interplanetary Saucers.'* Frontpage magazine article on April 7.

Time Magazine. 1963. *'Astronaut Cooper.'* Frontpage magazine article on May 24.

UFO Journal. 1967. *'Dr. James E. McDonald.'* Frontpage magazine article in January.

Vallee, Jacques. 1965. *Anatomy of a Phenomenon: UFOs in Space-A Scientific Appraisal.* NTC/Contemporary Publishing.

Vallee, Jacques. 1979. *Messengers of Deception.* Daily Grail Publishing.

Vallee, Jacques. 1988. *Dimensions.* Anomolist Books.

Vallee, Jacques. 1990. *Confrontations.* Anomolist Books.

Vallee, Jacques. 1991. *Revelations.* Anomolist Books.

Vallee, Jacques. 2010. *Wonders in the Sky.* Penguin Books.

Washington Post. 1952. '*Saucer Outran Jet, Pilot Reveals.*' Frontpage newspaper article on July 20.

Washington Post. 1958. '*Flying Objects Real, Psychiatrist Insists.*' Newspaper article about Carl Jung's belief in UFOs on July 30.

ABOUT THE AUTHOR

Chris Stafford resides in the San Francisco Bay Area with his wife and two children. Since 2002 he has owned and run a mobile surgical services company specializing in cancer, having spent most of his adult life in the medical industry. Chris was raised in Western Pennsylvania and received his college degree in philosophy, with a minor in science, from Saint Vincent College in Latrobe. He then did postgraduate studies at Wycliffe Hall, Oxford University in philosophy and comparative religion. Later he took advanced medical training courses at Harvard Medical School, Emory School of Medicine, and Medical University of South Carolina. Today, playing guitar and studying about UFOs are his serious hobbies.

.

www.ingramcontent.com/pod-product-compliance
Lightning Source LLC
LaVergne TN
LVHW021505080426
835509LV00018B/2404